FACILITATION

FACILITATION

A Framework for Psychoactive Exploration and Healing

JULIAN PALMER

Published by Anastomose

Cover Art by Suvi Parilla

Cover design by Maryna Arsenieva

Editing and Proofreading by Angus Donald and Clint Jewson

ISBN: 978-0-9925528-5-5

Dewey Number: 615.7883

First Edition

Printed by IngramSpark

http://www.julianpalmerism.com

Contents

Introduction

This book came to exist as I felt that there was a lot of quite theoretical and simple communications regarding the facilitation of psychedelics, that didn't go into the nuts and bolts of how to actually go about carrying out this work in a real sense.

This book doesn't highlight topics such as screening, integration and other information which I would perceive to be rather peripheral to what it actually takes to facilitate psychedelics.

I am largely self-taught, but have had many influences, friends and mentors who have assisted me along the way. This book is largely a communication of what I have learned, the mistakes I have made and what I consider to be the most important things to understand and consider in carrying out this work. What is communicated here is a particular personal view, which should contain within it, at least a few nuggets of gold for people who practice facilitation of all kinds. It will also be useful for the layperson to understand their own experiences and the realm of psychoactive consciousness itself.

My background is largely in sharing non-traditional

ayahuasca with people, starting off with the Australian acacias and Syrian rue, something which became my bread and butter.

My focus was in providing people with this medicine and this experience, without replaying traditional religious ideas about how to guide the space or sing traditional songs or enact religious rituals. And I facilitated these groups from 2002 to 2023, often quite intensively.

In 2013, I also began conducting cactus walks, a medium I imported from South Africa to Australia, where people take cactus containing mescaline and go walking in nature all day. I also have, over the years, conducted therapeutic sessions with people, whether that be one on one or two on one, with ayahuasca, MDMA, Ketamine, Iboga, LSD or Mushrooms. From 2000 to 2004 I also would have given smoked DMT to hundreds of people for free.

What I have come to understand most is how to create the human frameworks for people to engage deeply with the psychoactive space. And much of what I share here isn't "information" in the strictest sense, it is advice or understanding as to how these medicines work, how people can react to them, how to support people in these spaces and most of all, how to create these spaces. Much of the focus of this book takes into account the often more mysterious psycho-dynamics which occur in this space, and how our mental state, attitude and thoughts can affect other people when they are in such a sensitive and receptive space.

Our hyper-masculine society is very much orientated toward DOING, but in my experience, this space is more about non-doing. Rather than holding space, I'd say it is more important to GIVE space, a point I will reiterate in many different ways in this book. Much of what is most useful for facilitators to understand, is how they can shift their inner attitude and orientation, that makes people feel safe and comfortable to journey deeply.

My view is that, being a good facilitator is contingent upon how much work you have done on yourself, and that means people feel that you can be an anchor or someone that they can open up to and share with. This certainly doesn't mean learning a bunch of canned responses to common and difficult issues, which is actually not being emotionally present in the moment with your client and their in-moment needs. With all the talk of Artificial Intelligence taking the role of psychedelic therapists (yes, that is actually a real conversation!), the emphasis in this book is in bringing a human presence which is designed to support the intelligent process of your client, not to overtly determine their experience.

To truly empower your clients rather than controlling them, means being in tune with yourself, having an understanding of yourself and your client, so that you will know in that moment, the right thing to say to help your client make the most out of their experience, which often may not at all be obvious.

The space of psychedelic facilitation is very different to traditional psychotherapy, and in many respects my viewpoint is that the true therapist and healer in most of these contexts is the psychoactive plant or agent. The role of the facilitator in most instances is to provide a supporting role for the animistic healing intelligence.

That being said, there is a lot that you can do to support people, to provide the most responsive and conducive space for people to go deep and do the inner work that they want to do to effect change in their life. This book is an exploration of the many different non-obvious aspects of how to optimize being in a supporting role for someone else's journey with psychoactive medicine.

This book is the result of holding an online workshop and a real life three day workshop in facilitation, and realizing I didn't actually want to spend my time teaching what I knew about this subject in person, even though I found the process rewarding. So I decided to just download this particular understanding into the ever so untrendy written form, rather than a more ephemeral, and probably overpriced online course.

Chapter 1

Aligning Attitudes

As facilitators, perhaps the most important matter we need to take heed of is how we present ourselves to our clients, who are becoming ultra-sensitive to new layers of reality within themselves and also within us. Their incursion into often very strange and potent psychic material means that how we are BEING is generally much more important than how we APPEAR. For most professionals, how they present themselves is quite straightforward in terms of a professional appearance. In how they speak, there is generally a certain formal undertone that contains within it a certain nondisclosure of that which is too human. Such professionals largely don't need to be too concerned about their undisclosed thoughts, emotions, and states of being. However, when we're dealing with the ultra-sensitivity of people in the psychedelic state, we need to come from a place of profound self-awareness, in which we are not disturbing our clients or provoking them by any thoughts or feelings we may have at the time. Instead, we want to provide a human space most conducive for them to carry out the inner work most beneficial to them.

In our work with people, we want to present a centered human container and not put on any kind of performative act so that we are authentically congruent. The human we want to appear to be to our clients should also be consonant, to a large degree, with how we are generally in our private lives, as inconsistency implies too much performativeness. Sometimes, it can be that practitioners can confuse professionalism with formal distancing. A slightly impersonal and detached "professionalism" might be practiced by a dentist or accountant, but the situation is very different here, because we are present to people often engaging in their most vulnerable thoughts and feelings, and normally they don't know us well, or at all.

We must cultivate a space in which trust can develop, and someone you can trust is obviously going to be non-judgmental—or more accurately, non-condemning. But there are differing levels of readouts and judgments that people are going to make about you that might be difficult to ascertain, similar to how people might respond to us in any social situation. Perhaps your clients might notice your shoes look a bit old or that you didn't quite shave properly. They might notice that you make them feel uncomfortable in a way that they cannot put their finger on. You might remind them of an ex-friend whom they may not have treated well. You might have a smell that evokes a teacher they didn't like in school. If they are judging you—which they commonly will be, often due to their fear or apprehension—you don't want to be opaque in reacting to their judgment, but you do want to be secure in yourself and perhaps be a bit like Teflon. You definitely don't want to be a performative mirror, just reflecting whatever thoughts and feelings are directed at you and psychologically defusing them with any kind of practiced empathy, but you do want to let those thoughts and emotions not stick to you and inconspicuously fall away. This is where cultivating inner security and acceptance is important. You might notice your client subtly zero in on a weakness or two in you, but the point is, have you accepted your weaknesses? Have you come to terms with them? Or are you still pretending they don't exist? Your own self-acceptance and self-security, hopefully will give your client permission to also accept themselves as they are.

You also don't want to be judgmental, and that might be difficult when your client reminds you of a real estate agent who you feel wronged you, or of a person you used to work with who created unnecessary office politics. In a way, we need to stop pre-empting and prophesying where people are and where they will be. We need to freeze time to give our clients a sense that there is a space between time, to truly look at everything and assess everything in their lives. Because suddenly, in this deep space, your client may well realize what a petty Karen they may have been in their working life, or they may well be able to see how they have prioritized competitiveness in their life, or see their entitlement or prejudice. We need to be the one to give people space to see their issues, and we don't want to be the ones gloating in anything like petty *schadenfreude*. We want to encourage them to be in the space where they can have enough humility to get over themselves and "get it." We want to be glad that they have been able to feel free to cry and realize the harm they may have done and gain new perspectives on mistakes they may have made.

The professional attempts perfection, and of course, perfectionism is the cultic attitude of the shallow 5 star ethos of our time, and we don't really want to feed that beast. We are not supposed to be ideal role models of society or perfect people doing this work; we are on our own path, dealing with the madness and messiness of being human too. If you can give people a *sense* of your vulnerability or humanness—that you too go to the bathroom, pull hairs out from the sink, and sometimes burn toast—then it will make you appear more available, which is how you want to appear in order to create trust. The cult of the world idealizes appearing unavailable as having high status and at least "appearing" to be without flaws. Yet, by being in our flaws and accepting them, we can allow our clients to do the same.

Vulnerability is how people commonly connect, and yet it must not be performative or "professional vulnerability"—i.e., "This is the time for me to be vulnerable so you can connect with me." It should be a natural vulnerability, where you have nothing to hide, your palms are open, you are natural, not "authentic." If you have to remind yourself to soften your eyes, people will sense that. People would prefer to know where they stand rather than have a sense that others are hiding something or trying to be "better" than they are. It is probably better to imply weakness, rather than trying to stay strong. You are not supposed to be all strong; you are a person who is being there, who is being present. People want to know that you will understand and that you can hold them in a place of relative non-reactivity.

It is perfectly appropriate for you to be a flawed human being, but also, how can you share where you have come from to where you are now? That doesn't need to be your life story, and you don't need to have completely arrived at this mythical, psychedelically enlightened place. What is most important is HOW you weathered the storm, because the client will know that you have arrived where you are and that you can help them weather any storm you might encounter together.

What you DO NOT want to be, is "solid" on the outside and vulnerable or shaky on the inside, as people will generally feel that. Unfortunately, this is a common mode of the performative, egocentric self—the brave face or mask we present to the outer world. So many people present a steady or rock-like performative self, expressed both in their voice and how they appear in the world, which can often hide a frightened, childish, or confused interior. And this again means doing the inner work—perhaps the real inner child work—so that you can accept those aspects of yourself that are childish, frightened, and confused, and you've developed aspects of yourself that can support these emotions within your own being. Then you will be able to allow your client to be frightened, childish, or confused, and not judge them for it.

If there is an identity for a "healer," you probably don't want to be limited to that identity. Some people have issues about being a healer and how they may understand that. For example, some facilitators might have a past as a gang member or worked as a police officer, where they might have needed to be violent. You don't need an identity—you just need to do this work enough that you are confident in it and that you hold yourself with confidence. You don't want to have even a shadow of being an imposter; it's really time to get over that. Give it 80 or 170 hours of your time to work through this if you need to work through it. You want to be the opposite of an imposter, with the absolute right to be present and confident in your role.

There is no right way to facilitate, but you should at least cultivate sensitivity, so you can see how people respond to your state, how you are being, and what you are saying. You don't need to perform your vulnerability. You should simply be undefended and present as yourself in other people's presence, giving your attention to them with generosity, openness, and curiosity where appropriate.

Not everyone is safe to be around. People are defensive; they are attacking (especially those with serious trauma), but if you can defuse your client and let them know, in a deep sense, there is no space for any hijinks here, then they will understand that. You want to allow people to be able to come into their often chaotic interior self and be okay with breaking through what appears as a fourth wall at times, which is the performative egocentric self. People are more attuned than THEY think they are—and likely more than YOU think they are, too. When people feel you are not putting on a show and not "playing that game," they will be able to relax and come into a place inside themselves that is not playing the common worldly games. Then you might be able to truly allow them to open up and de-compartmentalize themselves a bit and see their own structures of being afresh.

In pretty much all societies, presenting yourself as being available may represent you as being of a lower status—because the king is not available, and the homeless person is infinitely available and present. You don't want to be like a homeless person, and you don't want to be like the king, or anywhere in between in terms of status. You want to be present and give people your presence and receptivity, so it is not a matter of being available or not. People are paying you to be present, and that means, largely, not looking at your phone or being distracted by other things.

Think about the people in your life who have made you feel most comfortable in their presence. What did they do? How did they act? What did they say? What was their interpersonal attitude? If you think about it, more often than not, it was simply their energy—how they showed up in the world—and everything they said and did emanated from their core relationship with themselves.

Because everything is amplified so much more in this space, you need to minimize the emanation of any body language and psychological cues that can distract people or cause them to be, in any way, "triggered" by you. Your attitude should not be one of obsequiousness—of fawning and putting oneself into a lower social space in the hope that this makes people feel safe. Neither should the attitude be one of having power, dominance, or a higher position over the individual. These attitudes tend to be common in many of the more "cultic" ayahuasca circles for example, where some individuals might let some level of power and the potency of their work get to their head. You will also find this attitude common in many practitioners of all kinds. I cannot tell you how many practitioners I've seen who are condescending and take the opportunity to "be the bigger person" and render me, the client, the lesser person—the person who needs their mighty healing help! The better practitioners have transcended all this worldly stuff, and so should you. I believe the most effective position is truly standing outside the whole realm of dominance hierarchy, or any kind of pecking order or modes of status. You are simply present—in relation to, neither above nor below, and you can acknowledge or be aware of the worldly games, but the space we should be co-creating is one free of all games.

You should be putting yourself in a simple human place, with an attitude of openness that is simply present and not "laying any trip" on people. The hippies in the 1960s developed that terminology from their use of LSD, whereby any imposition upon them was "laying a trip," which is a kind of infliction of one's own agendas, as people obviously do become very sensitive and attuned to these manipulations under the influence of psychedelics.

Most significantly, we need to be agenda-less—not wanting or needing something from anyone—and that also means not wanting to be liked. We should be most of all, in a space of allowance. We cannot stop people's projections, transferences, fears, and anxieties—even paranoia—but if we are aware, we can minimize how much these tendencies will affect the individual and help them to move through them, often by just letting them fall away and become redundant. If we are transparent rather than opaque, we are not giving the individual anywhere to hang their coat. Opaqueness is the way of the world. It is the realm of the known. We can then be embracing the mystery, but we should not be embracing the glamour of mysteriousness.

How we move should be like a knife through butter; there should be no opaqueness in our world. We should not even be navigating the world anymore in our movements. Neither should we be focused on our clients too much, especially in a one-on-one or two-on-one session. You want to be giving a rounded, 360-degree presence, not an angular confrontation. If too much focus and presence are applied to the client, it can become suffocating and claustrophobic for them. People are not often used to much attention or presence given to themselves. Very often, even friends or family are so involved in their own story that they don't give much attentive or listening presence. Sometimes such presence and attention can be awkward for people, and sometimes absolutely refreshing, or a bit of both.

You want to be in yourself, receptive but not overly so, as you don't even want people to relate to you too much. I would say in this space, there is a kind of Tao or Zen of being nothing, being nobody, but also somebody. Someone who is present, who is available, who can be asked for tissues or water, or someone who knows when to provide you with tissues or water.

One of the best ways to become better as a facilitator is to experience being facilitated. Then you will see how ungraceful movement can really put you off. Then you'll see in yourself how dialed-up your attention to detail is, and how attuned you are to implicit attitudes, thoughts, and feelings in the space, and you will also see what you find annoying or unnecessary in others and in the space itself. You'll often see how applied techniques or assumptions about the therapist's power or ability or desire to control where you are at, can really often get in the way of your flow. Generally the mind does want to control, and control is the way of the world. For this work to be most effective, I believe we have to encourage people to lose control and stop controlling or determining people in any way, and just let them surrender to the mystery and truly give them permission to do so.

I've taken medicine with all kinds of people—from all of the ayahuasca churches in Brazil, to ceremonies in a large villa in Ibiza, to ayahuasca in posh Melbourne suburbs, to mushroom groups in South Africa. Even if I didn't like the group or the ceremony, I learned something about what I liked and what I didn't like.

But also, you can learn a lot by seeing one-on-one practitioners of healing, such as therapists and bodyworkers, and observing what you find does work in their approach and what doesn't work. Personally, I like to experience many different modalities and approaches and see if I can find helpfulness within them. Many people I find get a bit stuck in their unique modality or preferred way of working, but I recommend branching out and seeing why people do what they do, and discover what you like about their manner and attitude. More often than not, it's easy to find therapists who have issues with how they present themselves and how they are with their clients.

Cultivating sensitivity and awareness is not necessarily an easy task in our often brusque and crude intersocial paradigms. Perhaps most of all, people want to find someone who demonstrates care. Often, what people are lacking is care for themselves—essentially love for themselves. If you can give people considerate attention, a window can open up into love at times. As healers, we don't need to love our clients, but we shouldn't repress or hold back love if it's present. And that doesn't mean long hugs, or even that hugs are necessary at all. Most fundamentally, it means being in the space of namaste—not in a schmaltzy, externalized West Coast manner, but in the true recognition of the divine within and honoring that within others.

This work is often messy, and you don't want to make all the pieces neat and tidy, and people don't really want you to make them neat—they essentially want the internal messiness to be allowed and accepted in their outer field. People will sometimes regress to inappropriate and childish states, where they will test boundaries. We need to be in a space where people know playfulness is okay and also that it's allowed to be expansive around you, and that you will not try to limit that expansiveness. Again, it all comes back to not being controlling or trying to determine people's experience.

The psychedelic experience can obviously be very strange and inexplicable. Even though people know I am very experienced and am generally considered a bit "out there," to say the least, people will often apologize or feel hesitant to share their reality, thoughts, or experiences. People will often seem to apologize, as if they are the only strange person, and I have to assure them that this is just another "day at the office" for me—and that they are not really so weird.

When people tell you their experiences, just listen. You don't need to jump on anything they're saying, comment upon it, or find some answers. But you could tell them you had a similar experience, or that you know a few people who have had a similar experience. We don't necessarily want to explain everything away that someone has experienced; they have their own path of finding and unwinding, unfurling what all this means to themselves over time. And of course, our insights and interpretations can be valid and valuable for our clients as well.

And yet, sometimes people will not even know what they've experienced, and you will have to coax it out of them. Their mind may not want to recognize truly transpersonal data beyond the control patterns of the known mind. I once had two Sundays in a row giving DMT three consecutive times to a man known to be stuck in his head, who would drink huge amounts of ayahuasca, and at the very most, only experience some geometric patterns. Each time he smoked DMT with me and a friend of his, we could see something profound was occurring, but his mind wouldn't let him talk about it. After many hours on both Sundays coaxing the fortress of his mind to surrender the truth, on the 2nd Sunday we were able to ascertain that during every DMT experience, he had been having some kind of intimate love connection with a female octopus-like being! And when he was finally able to let his defenses down, he was able to remember and acknowledge that this was what he was experiencing. Before slowly teasing it out of him, his mind simply wouldn't allow him to acknowledge what was actually occurring.

Chapter 2

Working with People

In many respects, we need to be at peace with people's accentuated projections, anxieties, and distrust of US. To some degree, this can be assuaged by recognizing their psychological tendencies and implicitly letting them know that we are not buying into their reactive thought patterns. It is not particularly useful to push back or become reactive to people's issues, that often don't have much to do with you. If they mistrust you, then they commonly mistrust themselves. If you can see that they are continually looking for flaws and faults in how you are, that is generally how they are imprisoning themselves. People are often prisoners of their own perfectionism and illusory ideas about how the world works, and so they are crippled to not do all that much, in case they make mistakes. With these people, I'd say it is useful to let them know that some mistakes are okay, we've just got to roll with circumstances, and actually DO the thing, which in this case is giving people highly potent medicines that can bring a very wide range of possible and potentially messy human states.

We must remember that projection in its most negative sense, is the individual projecting the shadow elements of their own psyche that they cannot easily own. When we really see and understand that and have a good eye for these tendencies, I think there is a natural response to have compassion for people who are unable to own their own shit. We don't have to react to people's projections, or tell people they are projecting. We really should be detached and let people do what they do, as we cannot stop them from projecting—and often they cannot do so, until they themselves become more responsible and mature.

I know one facilitator who gave up facilitating completely, as all the projections became a bit much for him, and his idea for a T-shirt was one that said, "Own Your Own Shit." We must remember that this is difficult for most people to do, but hopefully through this work, we can lead people to come to terms with their own shadow. This process can be very humiliating and humbling for people, and it should be a primary part of this work—having your arse kicked, becoming accountable for your own actions, and how you have been in the past. Associated with all of this are emotions of self-loathing, regret, fear of failure, low self-esteem, humiliation, unworthiness, shame, and guilt—often all mixed up and coming up to the surface all at once in different degrees. This is why medicine experiences should often be difficult. If such experiences are largely easy and positive, what we're probably seeing is some level of spiritual bypassing and a lack of accountability for one's present state of being.

Fundamentally, we must bring people back to self-acceptance and forgiveness—most of all, forgiveness of oneself and forgiveness of others. We should be helping people let go of resentment and any energetic charge that keeps them bound in negative emotion, especially toward those who have harmed them. People free themselves by letting these emotions go, and if you work with enough people, you will see people attempting to let go of grudges that imprison them, and to understand the long work that people go through in forgiving their perpetrators.

A lot of emphasis in this work is in helping the victims of trauma, but we must understand that the people who create the trauma are also in need of healing and they are often just as traumatized. Sometimes the line between perpetrator and victim is very thin, as the victim can very often become the perpetrator—perfect victims are also hard to come by too.

Perhaps one of the most challenging parts of this work is coming to terms with the extent of perpetration in our society—which is largely a fact that society hides from itself. It can be very difficult for perpetrators to find a place of non-judgment and acceptance, where they can come to terms with what they have done—and in doing so, realize that the trauma affects them as well. At the time, they may have acted tough or pretended they were invincible or able to act with impunity, only later to discover that these acts had affected them greatly.

Some of the people coming to you may be actively causing harm in the community. But the point is, if they have come to do medicine work, they are looking for healing. It can be difficult for them to find ANY place within society where they can openly air their issues without being condemned. We must remember that there are many people out there in society who are actively causing harm, who are far from wanting to seek any treatment or wanting help. For example, the people involved in satanic rituals, or the all too common chronic free-range psychopaths.

Many of these perpetrators clearly have etheric entities working through them, and it is these entities which are often inspiring how they operate much of the time. There may be subconscious or even relatively conscious contracts with these beings that are causing them to act in clearly harmful ways. Or, there may be more unconscious influences, this is particularly evident in cases of domestic violence in the presence of alcohol. Alcohol is well known to cause a lack of control, where the person may no longer feel truly in control of their actions.

Many people in our society have cluster B personality disorders—seemingly increasing so. These people often struggle to find treatment for these disorders (if they can even be called that), and there is a tendency in some circles to dehumanize people who are called narcissists, for example. All of us are human, and in many respects we are dysfunctional when we are not in contact with the primary aspects of ourselves that truly make us human. Attempting to develop a felt sense of empathy, for example, is what you would want the narcissist to do.

Rather than always categorizing and diagnosing people—in a sense condemning them to their supposedly incurable personality disorder—it is perhaps more important to take people as they are. We are going to get the best results with people by recognizing their humanity and treating them as human beings, and not buying into any manipulation or tendencies they may have. That being said, some people you will not want to keep working with; as the associated drama and difficulty around them might become too much.

In this day and age, people are commonly in love with their diagnostic labels, and for many people, these labels can serve as a way they can abnegate responsibility for how they are. At times, we may want people to move into a surrendered place where they can admit a dysfunction and just look a bit closer into the intricacies of how they are the way they are.

The facilitator should be able to create a space that allows the sociopath to "switch off" their manipulations and perhaps come into a sense of accountability and understanding of why they are the way they are. But truly, where healing begins for many people is at the ground zero of their own internal accountability, which they may have avoided, which involves just being where they are in themselves, feeling the shape and texture of their own suffering, and what that is telling them about how they know they need to change. People should be invited to stop their machinations of avoidance and deflection and just sit in their own suffering. For sure, psychedelics are often going to bring this chaotic pain to the surface, and many people are going to want to avoid that process of accountability with the inner self.

But it is only in facing their internal dysfunction

head-on—in the shape of visceral pain and suffering—that a person's overall system can recognize what their truest problems are and bring attention to how to solve them at a primordial level. Pain at any level can be perceived as a kind of warning system, signaling to the body to bring healing attention to that part of the psyche. When the individual blocks off the pain, and doesn't allow it to be felt, they prevent the healing process from reaching what isn't working. Many of these personality disorders and core issues in our society, such as addiction, represent the individual's attempts to numb their pain. When people do not feel their internal issues, they lose their co-ordinates and become liable to hurt themselves and others without even truly understanding what they are doing, and more importantly, why. Sociopaths don't necessarily intend to be sociopaths, but their internal system of self has shut down in all of its different parts and is often not able to be accountable to itself, due to lack of communication between these different parts of the organism.

These SSRIs and many psychiatric drugs, such as antipsychotics, also numb the pain for many people, closing off the emotional aspects of the self so that little emotional processing can occur. We must understand that psychedelics are catalysts for mental and emotional processing, allowing connection between the parts of the self and the natural and human world. This is why we must endeavor to be as neutral and sensitive as possible, to allow these repressed aspects of consciousness to make contact with the outer world and also possibly us.

A lot of healing lies in surrendering to how the

emotions want to be in the body and a release of the usual attempts to suppress, circumvent, or mentally manipulate emotional responses. In deep emotional processing, people forgo the usual social contracts and constructs and become very raw. Even just being in these states of emotional processing can be very humiliating and bring about a great deal of shame. This is why it is important that the facilitator knows what it is like to be brought to one's knees, in all the shapes and shades of how that occurs. And we should be allowing people to be on their knees—no longer standing in the world, but surrendering on the ground, not yet fallen, but assessing their situation afresh.

When someone is sitting in their core shame, not insulated from it by their ego or mind, having to acknowledge that something within them is fundamentally wrong, this is the first step toward creating change and healing. It is a very hard thing to do because you must accept the terrain of brokenness and own up to being in that, too. You should be able to empathize with them, have reference points to know what it is like to have this chaos of thoughts and emotions coming to the surface—and for what it means to own up to your own dysfunction in a pure way, that doesn't mask or explain away what the person knows isn't working for them. And there is another primary place we can remind people of also, a primary place within themselves which is not broken, which is incorruptible and pure.

Much of the time, all you can do is just let these processes take place. To some degree, the individual may be overwhelmed and overloaded with enough impressions and data that they will not be able to handle much more from the "outside" world. That being said, at times it is good to give the person a felt sense of coordination with another human being, so they can pause and get their bearings. And if they become upside down or sideways, you can just be upright and present to them the right way up for some time, being grounded on the earth like a rock, before releasing them back to the processes they were involved in—hopefully with a better understanding of what their human baseline can be.

Sometimes people can get stuck in loops, and this is where they might need help to get out of their loops. However, what I discovered when working in psychedelic emergency services at festivals, where people had overdosed on psychedelics, was that often they were in a completely different space altogether. There was normally no way to bring them out of their trance or their loop, and you just had to be there for them until they did "come back" into their body. Sometimes people can be in a very crazy space, repeating the same words again and again, and then suddenly come back into normality and stop and say "I'm back" or equivalent words, then in a very sudden way, appear normal again.

Many people who want to take psychedelics will commonly say that their primary issue is one of not wanting to lose control, which tends to tell us how important they understand it is to them, that they do lose control. What tends to happen when people do lose control is they realize it was okay after all, and the world did not end—though there might be a bit of collateral damage. Certainly, this extreme loss of control generally only happens with higher doses of ayahuasca or mushrooms, for example, but some people can be much more sensitive to the substance than you think they will be. It can all be a bit too much too soon for some, and they can go into a kind of shock and an inability to process. In these cases, it seems the individual can go completely out of their body, while some basic physical functions remain —while other processes still occur in other realms and places. Yet, often the individual will be so "far out" that they will not remember a thing. That being said, I have seen completely radical healings from very deep trauma and issues occur in this space, where an individual does completely let go.

Often there is not much you can do to assist such people, because they will not be able to take much on board, and they will be locked in their own process. Often there can appear to be a processing that is occurring, then a let go, and hopefully there can be epiphanies and realizations—profound "AHA!" moments of self-understanding taking place within the individual. Then we must come back to respecting the innate intelligence of the individual and empower them to know how to find their own rudder, and also to come back to the truth in the medicine. Sometimes the chaos and madness coming out of people is a purge of this madness and dysfunctionality that is being released from them.

In general, if we provide too much guidance to a group or an individual, they are not able to find their own guidance systems. Many people in our world are just lost. They don't have their own maps. Their own maps and guidance systems may have been taken away from them in childhood, were never developed properly, or maybe they were in a cult or religious group, in which they gave over their own autonomy.

It is only in giving someone space whereby they can discover their own guidance systems and their own intelligence. In some respects, you could say that any form of healing is simply allowing intelligent flow to return to the areas where there are blocks. Some more "new-agey" circles might talk about "holding space," but space cannot be held, as this implies we are bringing an agenda of holding and control. We want to create space for the individual to find their own flow, their own intelligence, to trust in themselves again, to find their own feet and their own head.

Of course, there are different levels of interference and confusion for the individual, and many elements within society that want to kneecap people's sovereignty and take them off their natural path. What we want to do is encourage the individual's own flow and therefore natural intelligence to come to the fore. As the individual realizes that they may have been off track, again, humiliation or shame can come into the picture, and it may often manifest as regret.

The facilitator, in an ideal sense, should be someone who has emerged out of the chaos of their own inner process and has a good grip on their own inner compass. Because if you don't have that grip on your own compass, how can you prompt other people to find their own compass and bearings? If you haven't been through "ego death" multiple times, how can you expect your clients to be able to safely let their "ego" die in your presence?

What we'll often see in the case of "ego death" is a great deal of fear that comes up for individuals, as the body and awareness can send signals as if it were physically dying. Then, it is important to reassure the person that they are not going to die, that they are fine, that they are safe, that you are not going to let them die, while also allowing them to surrender to the process where they can truly "let go." And then in that let go, therapeutic processes can occur beyond the mind, where the client's inner child may be able to process pre-verbal issues or even birth trauma. Often it is a just a matter of time, of providing reassurance and consoling, until the wave of fear or resistance inevitably passes.

We are all in varying degrees of life stages and processes, and hopefully we're at least heading in the right direction and yet many people are not. People who are heading in the wrong direction will often have to stop, work through their own disorientation, and realize they have been going the wrong way. This is huge for them, because suddenly all the people and environments they were traversing may no longer be so relevant to them. Then they have to navigate new environments and new people, and this is of course, the catalyzation of change. It can happen in one night that an individual can pull off their mask of being a shallow consumerist doll and realize that divine consciousness is real, and almost instantly give up many belief systems and shallow assumptions about reality. It can be very difficult to change your friends, your career, and your life as you know it. This is why time and space for integration is so important. Yet the individual will navigate this process themselves, with assistance from those around them, and they do not always need professional help with integration.

Chapter 3

Steering This Work through the Mystery

Different people have different approaches to this work, and different people will respond better to some approaches rather than others. My personal approach is relatively hands-off. I like to empower people to do the work themselves. I believe that especially when you are working with these agents from nature, such as ayahuasca, mushrooms, cactus, or iboga—that THEY are the primary healer and people are coming forward to experience the healing powers of nature, first of all. Then your main role is to support the animistic therapist and healer. I also believe in the inner healing intelligence of the human body and psyche, which wants to come into balance and alignment, if the elements preventing that healing are relinquished.

In the work I do with people, I always give respect to the animistic intelligence and give it space to come in and do its work. I could not conceive of doing this work without having an understanding that we are working with conscious and intelligent agents who are the primary teachers and healers, and furthermore, having a conscious relationship with these allies in the natural kingdom. Having that relationship, you understand how much power these medicines do have generating these mind states in people, and actually it is possible for the medicine to turn the volume up or down or even bring its own consoling and calming qualities to people who might be resisting or having difficulty with the space. But the main thing I like to do is to truly encourage people to listen to the voice of the medicine, which is always going to much more attuned and more able to say the right things than any human. We need to be able to trust the medicines, and the challenges that might be brought to people, and often this only comes from experience, by seeing how these medicines works with people moment to moment.

Early 21st-century "science" has a great deal of difficulty accepting the intelligence of these psychoactives, as this goes against the dogma of materialism, yet communion with these sentient agents of healing is simply what most every experienced researcher reports. When it comes to iboga, people will commonly report meeting and talking to the iboga plant spirit. Occam's razor (used without prejudice) tells us that the simplest answer is most likely to be true. There is not a simple or elegant explanation as to how a plant like iboga works that is as elegant and lines up with almost everyone's experience and the basic indigenous understanding of these plants—that they are conscious agents of healing. Experientially, that much is obvious to those of us who work seriously with these plants. Therefore, I don't attempt to prioritize any therapy or dialogue and largely give that work to the plants to carry out, who are able to carry out this transverbal therapy most effectively.

This issue is further confused because many dogmatic modern-day folks consider synthetic psilocybin to be the same as natural psilocybin from mushrooms. Yet, all of the people who are seriously into psilocybin mushrooms talk to the mushrooms and listen to the mushrooms. What's more, the real experts recognize stark differences between mushroom species. Psilocybin is not psilocybin, just as DMT is not DMT. Everything depends on the source of the molecule. Very experienced people, almost without exception, know this.

The issue with synthetic psilocybin, as with any synthetic substance, is that a guiding principle simply isn't embedded within a natural intelligence. Certainly in any synthetic substance there are still guiding principles within its "anima" (or animating intelligence), but they just don't have much maturity or a solid grasp on human realities, that the classic entheogens who have worked with human beings for many thousands of years do. The excuse people have for using synthetic psilocybin is that natural psilocybin cannot be measured as accurately. But actually, natural psilocybin is very easy to dose consistently if you know what you're doing.

The basis of how I work, is that the teacher or healer is primarily the plant entheogen, which is carrying out the healing work deep in the human organism, in ways that we can only just begin to understand directly ourselves. Therefore, we are present to support the person as they go through the processes that the medicine is catalyzing. From the moment I first connect with the client, I want to ensure their surrender to the process, that they trust the plants and they trust the space, and I aim to bring in presence and all the different elements so they truly feel safe to let go.

That being said, we can also inspire the client to engage in what is present for them if they are not actually engaged in their own inner work. For example, we can get them to do breathwork, focus on parts of the body, or assist them in engaging with a particular trauma or mental or emotional framework. We can enable dialogue with different parts of themselves. But for the most part, few people are going to be "stuck" and not processing anything; most people are going to be busy processing what is on their plate. When people are frozen and stuck or anxious or resistant, then our job is to unstick them and allow them to let go of their mind and ego, which is where the most powerful work can begin—and why entheogens work so well in the first place, as they can allow this type of let go where deep processes can occur as if automatically. If we are focused too much on therapizing our clients, they can go too much into their minds, and get caught up in psychological catchphrases and cliched themes and modes of the therapeutic environment, which could take them outside of their often delicate felt sense of self and lived experience. To my mind, the deepest healing will always occur in the deepest let go, and so we should encourage this let go, and not embark on some "hunt for healing" as you often would in a space of back and forth talk therapy.

Different plants work very differently. Iboga tends to be very communicative. Ayahuasca can be quite visual, and there can be communications within that, but there just might be geometric patterns also. All these agents commonly bring about a reckoning with the interiority of the self, as the chaos of the mind and emotions is brought to the surface, cleansed in the washing machine of process. Psilocybin tends to be a communicator—an agent of expansion and also journeying. Sometimes the tryptamines can be agents that bring in visitors from other realms. Mescaline from cactus tends not to be visual, but more emotional and mental, enhancing the self with somatic self-awareness and clarity of insight.

People who have engaged in therapy will commonly tell you that one of the primary benefits they have had from therapy is simply having the space to talk, and a listening ear, and the insights and feedback of the therapist are a bonus. A facilitator's feedback during a psychoactive experience should be minimal in my opinion, unless you can really feel the client is on the verge of an "AHA!" moment that you can catalyze. If you are applying any technique to your client, they may feel you are wooden and not in the moment with them and their process, which is very personal and unique. You may also appear detached from them if you are "therapizing" them.

Generally, an hour or so after the session is when I would recommend that you can really begin to talk with the client about what has happened, with another check-in a day or two later, and then one or possibly two weeks later, followed by weekly check-ins via text or voice notes for another month or so, and further calls if necessary. I like to include the price of an hour's debrief in the experience, and further hours can be billed separately, whereas texts and check-ins are just part of the duty of care, and actually, you'll just want to know how they are going. Often, you'll need to check in with them and find out, as they may not always tell you what is happening. I personally like voice notes and not being TOO formal, with a clear end and beginning to the integration. Some people, however do not need to be checked in on continually after their experience.

It is important to have boundaries around your time and not give too much time to clients unless they are paying for it. Though sometimes, it is good to go to 60 minutes in a talk without charging them for it, that's just my take, rather than being a hawkish lawyer charging by the minute. I generally charge a fee that accounts for the kind of support I'm willing to give after the session.

My belief is that sometimes there needs to be a working plan forward for the client, a certain amount of guidance, which might represent books to read, practices, or even supplements. For example, I once recommended Bravo Yoghurt to a client, which was very expensive for her, but she bought it and it healed her candida. Another male client I guided to understand that it was through his addiction to pornography and ejaculating too much, that was flattening his life force. I then recommended him to practice masturbation without ejaculation and to cultivate the male sexual energy.

I once had a client who took MDMA and needed a very large dose. This is something that I have found quite a few times—that some people have blocks, and you can overcome these with a very big dose and clearing of any interference that may be preventing the MDMA from working. If MDMA doesn't work for people at all, that's a good sign they have strong interference which is preventing the MDMA from working. A dose that works for them, may be anywhere from 400mg to 600mg of MDMA. Any more than this is really not necessary, and even those dosages could be very dangerous, especially with older people and those with weaker hearts. I used to know an older man who died overdosing on 500mg of MDMA. However, fit people under 40 SHOULD be okay. For most people, you would not want to give them more than 200mg of MDMA, as it is likely too risky, and I know one therapist who doesn't go over 120mg.

During one MDMA session with a woman client, she began screaming in a blood-curdling manner and began manifesting in a clearly demonic manner reminiscent of *The Exorcist*. When she later spoke to her therapist, who was apparently a bit of a dabbler in psychedelics (but considered himself an expert), he told her that he thought these manifestations were "unexpressed manifestations of childhood wounds" and "projections of the unconscious."

Clearly, this was some sort of numbskullery, as how could he presume to know? I think it is very unwise to impose your views on your client. To myself and my client, these abstruse viewpoints didn't make sense to either of us. It was evident to both of us that some possession was occurring. I didn't feel like I was imposing a viewpoint on her—it was just my considered opinion and her experiential reality. Luckily, she was open-minded enough to undergo a series of exorcisms under ayahuasca with a practitioner who specialized in that and made a lot of progress in addressing her CPTSD, which she eventually largely healed with judicious usage of psilocybin, cactus, and MDMA.

Rick Strassman, during his pioneering DMT trials in the 1990s, realized he didn't have the right to tell people that their experiences were not "real." I have only met three people in the global psychedelic scene who are very experienced and who disbelieve in the beings and interdimensional phenomena, and to be honest, they often come across as rather glitchy. Everyone else has either come to terms with the earth-shattering nature of the visitations, the transpersonal phenomena and privately accepts these as valid, while publicly many people may sit on the fence.

With ayahuasca, for example, these transpersonal states are just what you expect to occur. A lot of it is inexplicable and not easily explainable at all, and again, that is normal. Obviously, you shouldn't be determining anyone's experience for them, but letting people come to their own conclusions and guiding them to their own internal logic and feeling senses.

I consider telling people that entities are some kind of manifestation or hallucination of the inner self to be a form of malpractice, as it imposes ideological viewpoints onto someone's "lived experience." IF there were some good books or theories about this issue that actually stuck and resonated with the general community, then this sort of viewpoint could have some validity. Instead, we have rather flimsy arguments and theories from characters such as James Kent, whose ideas are not going to assist anyone in interpreting the great mystery. I don't know any practicing psychedelic therapists who take James Kent's theories seriously at all.

What we are actually facing is the rational or logical mind not wanting to accept the reality of phenomena that it doesn't understand. The mystery is our overwhelming experience. Some people have a tendency to impose insufficient theories or stories for the whys and hows of existence because uncertainty and surrender to the mystery is much more challenging. Rather than just consoling people with knowns, we need to make them more comfortable with this uncertainty and let them exercise these muscles, and eventually, they will generally find great solace in this level of surrender. We don't need to tell people that the expansive and transpersonal reality is real, because that is what they are experiencing. Our role isn't to tell people what reality is or isn't, but to allow them to unpack and understand what has happened to them, to the best of our ability.

Some people are "going to see the light" and get it right away and not need to overcome any cultural belief systems. Quite commonly, you are going to have atheists become "believers" in just a few moments. What you don't ever see is people realizing it is all just their brains manifesting this, or that the "hallucinations are all a trick of brain chemistry." It would make sense if something were actually true that people would naturally have realizations about it, as it would have gravitational weight of what is actually the truth. You never actually see people realizing it was all in their head, yet to some degree people can dismiss it all as "just a trip," but this appears more like a cultural artifact. Instead, what you see is people slowly (or more likely quickly) coming to terms with the nature of the mysterious, the expansive, and the multidimensional reality.

And much of the power of psychedelics, in my opinion, is not just that they expand the brain's capacity, but that they show us that there is a greater and wider context of reality. The colors that people see, the geometric patterns, are all primary information infusing into a person's awareness. When people do experience these different beings, they realize on a deep level there are broader dimensions of existence, which gives the individual a lot of headroom and a wider teleological perspective.

One time, I gave a one-on-one session with DMT from acacia, and Syrian rue to an Oxford-educated publisher of a well-known newspaper. He later wrote that he didn't come to any conclusions on the nature of God, but his experience of different beings, which he could interact with and be inspired by, was just as powerful, giving him the sense of there being "something more", which was greater than himself and that experience gave him a lot of perspective and insight into a vaster reality than he had experienced before.

Chapter 4

Touch and Human Relationship

There are of course, many different approaches when it comes to touch. Some facilitators don't like to touch their clients, while others may rock people in their arms and mother them. My general approach is to minimize touch of any kind and to only touch people if they need grounding or help people to come back to their body during a difficult experience.

Touching people on the hands and feet is probably the most non-confrontational way to touch the human body. In both the feet and the hands, there are acupressure points and reflex points which can help smooth out people's experience and these points become very obvious when you begin to apply pressure to them.

A good example of an acupressure point you can easily use with people is the Large Intestine 14 point (Hegu), between the thumb and forefinger, on the muscular webbing on the highest part of the muscle bulge. In most people, this point will feel slightly sharp, yet some gentle pressure and holding there can really help to bring people back to their body, relieve anxiety and move energy.

The basic premise of reflexology is that the hands and feet holographically reflect the entire body, and that you can reach and touch the whole body through the feet or hands. However, what I find most useful is not to just look at the physical body in the reflex points, but the energy, body and the chakras. I generally find that people have nodules and sore spots along the bridge of their feet if they have an obvious blockage in that chakra. Most people are going to benefit from you finding the point of the heart chakra, which I have found to be clearly located on the actual bridge of the foot, across from the physical heart reflexology point.

You can find that point in most people quite easily, because it is generally quite pronounced, and then you can hold that point gently for up to a minute until it releases, and the nodule dissipates.

It could be worth doing a reflexology course if you are not confident in finding different reflex points, but there are many maps online that will tell you exactly what part of the foot aligns with what part of the body. With some practice, you'll find it to be quite precise. For example, people who have issues with their reproductive systems will often have very pronounced nodules below their Achilles heel, where the various reflex points for the reproduction system are.

People with back pain can experience some relief if you massage along the bridge of the foot, but it is only with practice that you will know what to do and get the feedback and results. That is why I recommend people actually train in some modality of bodywork, particularly one that focuses on acupressure points and meridians, such as shiatsu or tui na (Chinese bodywork). Thai massage or other forms of massage that focus on the muscles are perhaps less useful.

For myself, I did a short course in shiatsu in the late 90's and began to learn the meridians and how to clear blockages in people's energy fields. When I was learning, it was startling practicing on one of the other students and literally seeing the pulses in the liver meridian open up for her, which looked like strong electrical twitches in her muscles.

When you have a basis for practicing, then you can use your intuition more. The issue with a lot of body-workers is that they never relinquish the technique and only apply the technique, rather than stepping out of the technique and finding the real spots and issues. My personal style is to truly tune into the body and then to intuitively know where the spots are, to hold them until they release so that people get relief, being sensitive enough not to cause too much discomfort, as these places of holding and contraction are often quite tender and sore.

If we lived in a sane world, all of us would learn how to give each other bodywork—to relax our muscles, align our bodies, and come into our center and spirit more. Touch is a significant gift that we can give to each other —if only we would apply it and give ourselves permission to do so. This is something especially important to share with our significant other and loved ones.

If we lived in a society where we all "groomed" one another and swapped massages, we would live in a much healthier society. As it stands, most of us struggle to find the money or time to have consistent bodywork, which are often considered a luxury in our society. And it can be a struggle to find good practitioners, perhaps because we treat other professions to be more prestigious, and highly attuned people may not find their way into becoming bodyworkers. I also find that most good practitioners have difficulty finding someone as skilled as they are to treat them properly.

One of my most profound bodywork experiences was with an American woman trained as a medical doctor. With her knowledge of anatomy and her incredible sensitivity, the feeling of being in good hands and being touched so respectfully created an enormous amount of safety and feelings of well-being, which just compounded on top of one another. Such rare people who truly know and understand the body can create an enormous amount of pleasure and well-being through their healing touch.

Consent is a bit of a buzzword in our present day culture. However, it is important to realize that some people don't like to be touched, and it is generally a good idea to ask people if they are okay with being touched, ideally before the session. If you ask people for consent in real time, they might feel pressured into saying yes.

Touch is not a big deal in many modalities where they don't necessarily even ask for consent. For example, in yoga or Pilates classes, the teacher will commonly touch the client to align their body and guide them. However, it may not be appropriate to touch some people. For example, I have worked with a Middle Eastern woman who wore a burqa during the ayahuasca groups she came to. I have also worked with Middle Eastern women who come from a culture where they would normally wear a burqa when engaging publicly within their society. Such a woman would not be used to a man touching her under any circumstances and may, in a heightened state of consciousness, respond with conflicting signals and mind states which would not be helpful.

If you are a man and you are working with female clients, it can be that touch can bring a bonding energy, or involuntarily trigger her to feel a kind of bonding—which may imply romantic attraction, or even sexual attraction—in a way that she may not be able to have any conscious control over. If you are a woman working with male clients, you should already be generally quite aware of how easily men can be stimulated or aroused, and that this involuntary arousal can be amplified when being in the psychoactive state. So it is definitely worth paying attention to the clothes that you are wearing also.

Overall, it is important to keep in mind, that people are in very sensitive and susceptible states, outside of their ordinary mental state. It is important that you, as a facilitator, have come to terms with touch as a medium, not as something that connects to sexuality at all, and in most cases, acts to console, heal, and align the body. However, we must remember that people are generally not in control of their bodies' own reactions. A male bodyworker friend said to me how common it was to ask his heterosexual male clients to turn over onto their back after being massaged while facedown, and he said the common reaction in their body, which they are normally very embarrassed about, is an involuntary erection.

The point is, if we can remain in our center and be in a nurturing space, touch is a primary and pure medium of communication—of giving comfort, support, and healing energy. Touch in western society is often quite sexualized. For example, men touching each other is often considered homosexual, and I once had a friend who was gay bashed because he touched another man on the hand in an act of friendly consolation. If we are working in a western context (or any cultural context for that matter) it is worth keeping in mind people's sensitivities, but also not be imprisoned by cultural norms. We know that touch often has been sexualized in western society, but actually it really shouldn't be, as it isn't in many cultures.

On the other hand, my personal approach is to only really touch people if they truly need assistance. I find putting a hand on the back of the heart and holding a steady presence there can be very supportive. This is more a hand of presence and energy than a physical hand. You should be steady, with your thoughts aligned and grounded when doing this.

It is useful, I believe, for facilitators to understand the basics of energy work. For myself, I did that by doing Reiki Level One, which is a very accessible course you can do over a weekend for not a large amount of money. After doing that course, you should be able to feel and transmit energy and have some awareness of these levels of reality. Mainstream society hasn't yet come to terms with these layers of reality, which are experienced by the individual and not easily measured scientifically.

I also find tapping the top of the breastbone in front of the thymus gland to be very helpful, which activates the function of the thymus gland. You can try this on yourself to see how it feels. It should feel stimulating, calming, and warming to the body. You should feel more present. After this tapping, the thymus gland should produce more T-cells and become more activated. More esoterically, the thymus gland is connected to an energy center, which different people call different things. Some people call it the “high heart” or the “soul seat,” or some call it “the happiness spot.” Different people have different interpretations of this energy center and what it means. I like to think of it as a center where we feel our connection to everything, and by tapping this center, we can begin to feel more connected and release any fear or tension we may have.

There are also tuning forks for the body, which I find are most effectively applied directly to the breastbone in front of the thymus gland. These tuning forks are not too small and not too large and often have a rubber ball at the tip, which you can apply to the body. The Otto 128 Hz tuner from biosonics.com works well, as does the 136.1 Hz Om tuner. You can also place the tuning forks on the back of the heart and on top of the heart itself.

If people are in a chaotic space, the tuning forks can really bring people right back into themselves and clear up a lot the confusion and chaos, something I have experienced myself with the tuning forks. I believe they are an essential tool for people working with psychedelics, as they are so noninvasive, people love how they make them feel—which is much more relaxed and centered. However, you have to be careful not to let people use them who don't know how to use them, as if they are hit too hard, they can quite easily go out of tune. Other places I like to put them are the top of the head, on the knee, and at the base of the spine.

I believe what is most fundamental in this work is having a basic understanding of the bio-energetic field and how it operates. Western culture, for example, is not particularly enmeshed in an understanding of the bioenergetic field, and cultures of largely European descent (such as Australia where I was born) tend to be more heady cultures—largely out of contact with the bio-energetic field. However, we are recently seeing more therapeutic mediums emerging which focus on healing the bio-energetic field, through energy work or allowing the body to shake and release stuck energy. Some of these modalities that come to mind are Pranic Healing, Spinal Energetics, Neurowave, Network Chiropractic and Integral Energetics.

Wilhelm Reich, an Austrian contemporary of Freud, developed an understanding of orgone energy, consonant with Eastern concepts of chi or prana. One of his students, Alexander Lowen, developed bioenergetics designed to bring people to connect to their own bioenergetic field through certain physical poses and exercises. Bioenergetics was the forerunner to what is now known as TRE (Trauma Releasing Exercises), and was also highly influential to many other fields.

In John Pierrakos's 1990 book, *Core Energetics:*

Developing the Capacity to Love and Heal, he maps the chakra system as not just being spinning wheels as they are typically depicted in eastern viewpoints, but funnels that spin, with a front and a back section. He also began to map the human auric field based on his own observations.

A student of John Pierrakos, Barbara Ann Brennan, took this work a few levels deeper, especially with her two books, *Hands of Light* and *Light Emerging*, designed to be textbooks for spiritual healers. *Hands of Light* is very interesting and maps the chakras and layers of the auric field, and communicates how spiritual healing can occur by interacting with the auric field. But it is in her book *Light Emerging* that she presents her most startling observation—cords of energy passing between human beings, a kind of etheric bio-plasma.

I first encountered these two books when I was 18 years old and considered them at the time to be a kind of science fiction. Over the years, I came to see them as absolutely brilliant, but quite psychologically flawed works, as they posit such a thing as a normal human energy field and also a human reality where these energetic relations are occurring in a consistent manner. Barbara Ann Brennan never critiques society itself (at least not in those two books), nor mentions too much about malevolence —perhaps an indirect nod to Wilhelm Reich, who charged society itself as sick and paid for it with the destruction of his books, his technologies, and his life.

I do think some of these techniques and processes Brennan describes are very useful to understand the healing process—for example of enabling people to feel safe in relationship and aligning the Hara. Having an understanding that there are these metaphysical, horizontal dimensions of relationship, I think is vital for practitioners and for human beings to understand in general.

But to practice spiritual healing or "laying on of hands" doesn't require you to do any specific training, although of course any training in these matters is surely going to be valuable. Anyone can provide energetic presence and learn to give spiritual healing. For many people this type of healing is an inbuilt gift, or it begins to come through them. For many people, it is something that they are not even DOING at all; the healing is something that is occurring through them.

Our society is just beginning to come on board to want to understand spiritual healing, with various people and modalities beginning to enter mainstream society and gain some acceptance. My general feeling is that spiritual healing is its own modality, and perhaps it is best that people approach it on its own terms. However, as a practitioner, it is perhaps the modality—along with a form of bodywork—that is going to be most useful to you in terms of practically working with clients.

However, it is the knowledge implicit in spiritual healing, that shows us that humans are primarily energetic beings that is I think very useful. Your increased conscious awareness of these layers of reality can provide your clients with a more aligned and respectful presence of awareness, that can give them a deeper and wider container in which to be experienced in and held.

Chapter 5

Tools

There are quite a few ways to influence people in their experience of going deep inside themselves. Probably the best way you can do this is through music. If you are going to start working with people in this space, you will want to start hunting for the music that you like and feel works best in the psychedelic space. Often, I find myself like a DJ, listening through albums and trying to find those golden tracks that really hit the spot. I really only like to play the golden music—the 5-star music that truly strikes a chord. It is also a good idea to swap playlists with your friends and recommend music to each other.

You want the music to bring people to focus within and likely don't want to play music that takes people too far outside of themselves. You will likely want to collect music that ranges in moods and angles, so that you can play the right track for every moment. You need to discover what music applications work best for you and what equalizer settings you prefer for your music. Different people also have different speaker setups they prefer, from a large dual-speaker setup, to portable Bluetooth speakers—set up by themselves as mono or otherwise in stereo pairs.

I find that much of the time, the best music for the entheogenic space is music that has been inspired by the entheogenic space or is deliberately created for it. Byron Metcalf's music is a very good example of this type of music. There is a lot of very interesting music that comes out of the psychedelic trance scene and its "chill stages," where ostensibly, people are there to "chill out." This genre has become its own respectable form, and I've been to a house party in London that had its own chill area with chill music—not so much being about chilling, but simply about enjoying and listening.

Then there is the neo-classical music—music that is contemporary in nature but composed and played with classical instruments. Ethnic or world music has never-ending interesting tracks that can add spice and fullness to the space. Then there is music coming more out of an ambient space—electronic compositions which are often quite subdued. And then there is the "new age" music, which might focus on instruments such as bells, gongs, chimes, and softer instruments and keys. Then there is also the devotional singing music—the various types of "kumbaya" music. There is so much sappy music coming out of the ayahuasca world; where one man singing and playing guitar is typical, and some of that music I find is great to play at certain points in the journey for people. But honestly, I wouldn't take that to be the only type of music I listened to in the space. In terms of ayahuasca music, there are some decent recordings of icaros as well. But personally, I wouldn't want to hear them the whole night, when there is so much nourishing music out there that you could play. Just by exploring Bandcamp or SoundCloud, you can find music that defies categorization, and often this music that doesn't conveniently fit into labels and it is some of the most poignant music.

There are also musical instruments that you can play; for example a drum or rattle can provide a repetitive soundtrack. Because this sound is organically created by a human, it is comforting that someone is present, and keeping a strong rhythm can help people to keep on track. I will only play a drum or shake a rattle for maybe 10 minutes maximum, and then maybe have some silence, and then perhaps play other music.

I've personally not gotten into rattles too much to disrupt negative energy or to clear people, but obviously, that is a thing. There are cultural connotations that come along with rattles, and to my mind, they are a bit opaque in their nature, potentially distracting, and more in people's faces than I would like.

But if you are proficient in musical instruments, then you can provide a whole soundtrack for people. I have commonly worked with people who play live soundtracks and use a range of instruments such as gongs, harmonium, didgeridoo, hang drum, crystal bowls, various chimes, guitar, pipes, and other string instruments.

What is particularly potent is if you can bring a very good didge player to play over people's bodies, especially over the chakras. I've found this to be especially effective deep in the ayahuasca space, but it is also brilliant in one's ordinary state to experience as well.

When people are journeying deep, you can affect them positively via their senses in only a couple of ways —through sound and smell. As I mentioned in the previous chapter, I try to avoid touching people. Taste is obviously not on the menu, and people are often experiencing an inner vision, so there's not much point in projecting videos on a screen, as that would likely only be distracting.

I don't use cheap synthetic incense sticks and rarely use any incense sticks at all. I sometimes use the thicker incense sticks from Nepal or Bhutan, which are generally made with a juniper base. Mostly, you have to use resins from plants, and that means burning those little charcoal discs and burning the resins on the discs. You also need to ensure you are purchasing high-quality charcoal discs, as the inferior ones don't light properly (or at all in many cases), and some of them light up too erratically.

Most people are aware of frankincense or palo santo, but not of the many dozens of incenses you can use from all over the world. The way I personally use incense is by burning the right incense at the right time, just as I am attempting to play the right music at the right time. These incenses are psychoactive and transformational in themselves, and they do have a stronger effect than many people may give them credit for.

Almost all cultures of the world have used incense to ward off evil spirits. I wouldn't say that you can completely rely on incense for this, but they certainly can help. Malefic spirits cannot be completely repelled by incense; but they don't like the sweetness of the incense, the way the smoke moves through the air, and the vibrations of the incense—which are of a plant intelligence in innate alignment. I'd say there is a spiritual element in the smoke as well, which the entities don't like from certain plants.

A lot of people treat palo santo wood as a cure-all for entity interference, and sure it can help, but it is not some sort of failsafe "weapon" in the way that many people believe. You're almost never going to exorcise people with palo santo alone. I'd say most of the well-known resin incenses have beneficial effects when it comes to the clearing of interference and stuck energy.

White sage is of course very nice and can be used for smudging over people. I've heard of ceremonies where that's the ONLY smell they use, and I personally think it would be very irritating to smell white sage most of the night.

Smudging (where you cleanse someone's body with the sage smoke) is sometimes very nice to do, but I think it is perhaps a bit overrated. I often find that the best time to smudge people is during the last quarter of their experience, when they are surrendered, and the smell of sage is nurturing, and people can welcome its cleansing properties in. I tend to think that when smudging people with sage at the beginning of a ceremony, its effects can "bounce off" people more.

What I recommend to people is to learn about all the incenses of the world—from all the different copals, benzoin, opoponax, all the different pines, sandalwood, damar, sandarac, elemi, and all the different powders from Bhutan, and so on. When you burn these incenses, feel what they do to you—what do they evoke? What is being communicated? How do you think they may help people clear and move past old energies?

I tend to think a high-quality Omani frankincense, burned at the right time—maybe when people are having a hard time—is a sweet reprieve and breath of fresh air. It is a reminder that life has created such sweetness from within itself. This type of smell takes us a little bit out of ourselves and brings us back to our senses, which is innately grounding. We are also, of course, returning to the aligned balance of nature.

Essential oils can of course be used too, though I personally find them to be more of a background hum than having the potent clearing quality you can find in resin incenses.

As well as incenses, there are various other olfactory tools you can use too. Sometimes I have used sprays containing essential oil hydrosols (the water-soluble parts of a plant) of Australian sandalwood—spraying them on people after a session, which they find very refreshing. Sometimes I have used various sprays containing essential oils and vibrational essences. These appear to work well to clear the space, and at times, I might spray people with them.

I have also used various products containing essential oils. Sometimes I may put a drop on people's wrists before the session as a kind of anointing. There are also other oil blends that you can put on people's palms so they can rub them over their body. These high-quality oils (often containing jojoba and other precious oils) tend to be nourishing and comforting for the body's largest organ—the skin.

I am personally appalled by "Agua de Florida," a common floral water brand used in the South American ayahuasca space, made with synthetic scents. However, I believe it may have a kind of morphic or symbolic power. There are companies such as Pureheart Alchemy in Australia, who make REAL Agua de Florida with real floral water and vibrational essences, which is a much better product. Again, I find it is better to give this to people toward the tail end of their journey or at the very end, to nurture their senses.

I am very much into flower essences, but have never much gotten into oral introduction of flower essences, gem essences, or any vibrational essences in the medicine space. I have worked with vibrational essences in the sprays and oils that I use. Certainly, you could make up custom blends of flower essences to spray around the room if you had access to a whole kit, or you could make your own flower essences for the space.

Chapter 6

The Medicines

To know the dosage of a particular psychoactive medicine, you really should know what a low, medium, or strong medicine experience feels like. You might also want to feel what TOO MUCH really feels like. In fact, I would recommend it, as long as you take precautions. If you are a serious explorer, you are going to have deep experiences that might take you far outside your comfort zone anyway. It is not always about the dosage you give to people either, as sometimes these more powerful experiences can be catalyzed by a relatively small dose.

There are many techniques for determining dosage, and some people like to dowse the dose with a pendulum. I no longer use a proper pendulum for dowsing, rather I use any kind of cable or implement I have around me—like a pen, or phone even. I have previously dowsed dosages for people, and have felt that was a good way to put my mind out of the way and sometimes I still do it.

You can, of course, use your experience and common sense and look at someone's body weight, ask them about their sensitivity to substances, consider what they want to achieve, and most importantly, ask them how deep they want to go. Asking the client may appear obvious, but many facilitators just standardize the dosage, and give everyone about the same amount. For example, many MDMA therapists may stick with 100–120 mg. However, I often give people 150–200 mg, especially those with a lot of MDMA experiences.

Body testing, or kinesiology, can also be used to determine dosage. You can hold someone's arm and get a yes or no for dosage, which is a well-known technique in kinesiology that anyone can learn. Asking someone's body is a kind of foolproof method of obtaining an amount to dose a person, however, I personally almost never use this method. These days, I just know the dosage, or a number comes into my head.

My approach with dosage is that you need to get the dose "just right." If the dose is not enough, then the person might be stuck in their head. If the dose is "too much," they may become too transpersonal, too challenged by too much data, or go too much in the slipstream of chaos, speedy intensity and let go, to really process what they need to.

I generally like to provide a dosage that puts people on the edge, so they can reach back into their awareness but also peer over the abyss if necessary. Then people can move into the transpersonal for a time, but also scour and investigate their own personal inventory in a space of "enhanced thinking," whilst also having a connection to the transpersonal.

In many respects, as a facilitator, a big part of your role is that of an expectation manager. People have all these ideas about what is going to happen. Sometimes the healing may happen in silence, "under the hood," and doesn't happen with any visions, fireworks or good feelings at all. Much of the time, it appears the plants are just entertaining us with visuals, similar to videos of dolphins swimming in the sea or jumping antelopes in Africa, or similar scenes that you might expect to see on a screen whilst at the dentist. With Iboga and Peyote, for example, some people can be astounded by just how cartoonish and outlandish some of the visuals can be, and these inner videos actually often may not represent any personal or transpersonal information, but just the plants wild play with a human.

Some people may just want to go into the purely transpersonal, and that's fine. The transpersonal is still, in a sense, a reflection of the personal. People who haven't established an ontological foundation in themselves for the transpersonal, may often have difficulty even reaching it. Of course, many people are stuck in their mind and ego, and you may have to use very big doses for them to crack the cage of control they have established in their fortress. It generally is the case when people begin taking psychedelics, that they start off needing largish doses, and as they become more experienced, they will often need less and less, as the organism doesn't need the bigger doses to break down any inner walls.

For dosing chemical substances like MDMA, I prefer to use vegetable gel caps. I have never put MDMA or any other substances into orange juice or other liquid mediums to dose. A lot of the time, it can be challenging to just obtain therapeutic grade substances, as a lot of the black-market substances are not up to scratch for therapeutic use. For example, obtaining MDMA that is made with care and consideration from safrole precursors, can be quite tricky at times. I don't at all rate any material made from the synthetic precursor PMK. Sure, it works and has a certain clarity to it, but it just doesn't have the warmth, dimensionality, and depth of the material made from high-quality safrole. Over the years I've known a few people who make MDMA, and there is a huge difference between people doing this consciously and with care, who can innovate techniques and processes, and people who are just out to make a quick and messy buck by following a simple recipe. When it comes to MDMA, much of the quality of your MDMA is going to be determined by the mind state and intention of the chemist. The better material is going to come from the chemist who is in it for the right reasons, who has a pure intention and takes care to do everything as carefully and consciously as possible. This better quality material should effectively have no comedowns on day 2 or 3. Whereas almost all of the MDMA made in the world is just made en masse without the necessary care and concern you truly require for therapeutic grade material.

A lot of the psilocybin mushrooms that are home-grown can be a bit sterile and not have enough oomph and spirit. So much is contingent upon who is growing them, and the mushrooms themselves are often going to reflect the needs and demands of the grower. Once I took a solid 5 gram dose of cubensis mushrooms from some shiny people types, quite surface and visual in what they valued, but who were nonetheless special people. The experience was more like 2 grams of what I was used to in mushrooms. It was still a visual experience, but the mushrooms just didn't have the get-up-and-go to transform my world, and not that much happened.

Over the years, I have reflected upon the nature of different batches of LSD, and it has always struck me how the LSD made by chemists reflects their worldview, the qualities of their humanity, the place in which they made it, and the materials and processes they used.

When it comes to the preparation of plant medicine, people have always wondered why my medicine was so potent and worked so well. Even people who brew medicine themselves or drink with many others cannot easily understand it.

I once had a situation in South Africa where some acacia tea was stolen from me after a particularly potent night, where experienced people said they just hadn't had medicine like this before. My friends joked that the people in the South African scene were probably looking in my bags, trying to find my secret recipe—perhaps a strange amulet made from a human skull or some other human body part.

Perhaps the main thing to understand, is that the quality of the plant medicines you serve lie in your relationship to these plants. In Amazonian traditions, you develop a relationship with the plants by dieting with the plants that you are working with. For myself, this generally just means drinking with the plant A LOT and developing a relationship with the plants in that space.

And in the brewing space, this means bringing that knowledge of the intelligence of the plants to the people drinking who may not have a relationship with that plant; giving space to the plants when serving the medicine and not taking that space up by myself. Humans are so caught up in overly simple ideas of "strength", but strength is largely just dependent on dosage. What is perhaps most significant is creating a medicinal medium reflective of the intelligence of the plant, which desires to make a conscious communication with the people who partake of it.

When it comes to making ayahuasca or an Acacia and Syrian rue tea, it really is just like making tea. Human beings always try to make simple things complex, as this is the tendency of the human mind. For many people, they cannot easily understand how such a profound thing could be so simple to do. Sure, there is a bit more to it than that, but it is actually a very simple process.

There is definitely something to be said for the energy you bring to making the tea. For myself, I try NOT to bring energy to the making of the tea or introduce my energy to it, as I believe that would be corrupting the purity of the plants. That means no ceremony, no chants, no crystals or trying to put something into the tea that wasn't already there.

I personally don't understand people who serve other people's medicine. A big part of the process of serving the tea, to my mind, is knowing the ingredients and nature of the tea. Generally, I pick the acacia phyllodes myself, and I often harvest the ayahuasca vine from someone I gave cuttings to many years ago.

When harvesting the acacia, this also means stopping and recognizing the plant as a living being, and asking the trees which phyllodes (leaves) or twigs I should take and I generally only take a small amount of phyllodes from each tree.

In that process of harvesting, there is an inherent respect and gratitude that is not particularly performative. I've never personally done anything much like leaving offerings or performing any kind of ritual. I believe the plants can feel how we regard and respect them, and I don't believe they want to be worshiped from a distance on a pedestal, but rather simply respected in present moment awareness.

In an ideal scenario, you would harvest your own plants that you have grown yourself, that you have a connection with, and that you have planted. However, not everyone owns land, or if they do, it's not enough land or in the right climate zone to grow psychotropic plants.

When making tea of ayahuasca or acacia, I am a big believer in using the purest water possible, ideally collected from a natural spring. I never ever use just tap water, and I would truly hesitate to even use reverse osmosis filtered tap water, which I consider to be a kind of dead water. And I will use a good acid source, preferably a non-corporate brand of apple cider vinegar, or maybe from lemons I have picked myself.

Then I prefer not to use too much heat when brewing, just allowing a few bubbles. The heat should not go much above 80 °C. My idea is not to change the pH level too much, to leave the plants alone as much as possible, not to interfere, and to just allow their essence to enter the water.

I generally do two "cooks" for 2–3 hours each time, then strain and slowly simmer down, and again, without many bubbles. Sometimes I do a third cook if I have time, as I do believe some more of the plants essence is drawn out in the third cook. If you are using a low enough pH, the third cook isn't actually going to pull many more alkaloids.

I prefer bigger cups than 30 ml or those of a normal shot glass, which might work well for traditional ayahuasca. For acacia, I prefer 60–100 ml as a standard dose, as I don't believe the acacia likes being concentrated so much, and it appears to compromise it or even destroy it in some cases.

This connection with the plants carries on into serving the tea to others. I often talk about the specific plants we are imbibing to participants and invite them to connect with them. In many respects, I am making an introduction from myself to the plants. This is why drinking with me, from medicine I created, is probably going to result in people having better contact with the plants than if you just found them and brewed them yourself.

With mushrooms, I really like the way of taking them with high-quality cocoa or dark chocolate. Chocolate tastes good and helps smooth out the come-on and any potential nausea. You can also easily make your own mushroom chocolate by combining cacao, cacao butter, and a sugar source of your choosing and then pouring the mixture in chocolate molds.

When taking cactus, I find the tea made from the fresh cactus is okay, but a bit strong to drink, and it tends to create a bit of nausea in some people. I prefer to use dried cactus powder, which is a bit annoying to dose.

The way that I do it is to put 20–35 grams of cactus powder into a cup of high quality apple juice, and then ask people to stir decisively and drink it all down quickly. This can be a bit messy and still has a strong taste for people who are unpracticed at doing this. If people wait too long to drink it down, the cactus absorbs the juice and becomes impossible to drink at all.

Of course, clear white mescaline sulphate or citrate or equivalent, extracted from the cactus, is superb if you can get it, and I have found the isolated mescaline to be a profound spiritual tool. There is certainly something about the clarity you can get from the extracted mescaline, that may make it a better therapeutic option than the cactus tea, powder, or extract.

Its long duration means that mescaline hasn't gotten the attention that psilocybin, for example, has received. In practice, it takes two hours to come on, and the actual peak of the effects may last from 4 to 6 hours in duration, after which time the client may not need so much attention.

I feel like a lot of deep internal work can be done with mescaline and breathwork in particular. Perhaps not for 5 continuous hours of breathwork, but forays of 20–30 minutes, then allowing mental and emotional material to come up and be processed with intention. Or you could go for an hour or two of breathwork. Of course, breathwork is just going to amplify the effects of any substance. I don't like to make it complex—just quick inhalations and exhalations in and out from my mouth as my body naturally does. I think it is one of those things that may appear challenging when you first start doing it, but once you exercise those muscles, it is not difficult at all to do for a few hours.

The advantage of mescaline is that it can truly allow deep inquiry into emotional issues, childhood issues, and our own intrapersonal communications. This can bring understanding and resolution deep within the organism. Tryptamines can often be more transpersonal, whereas mescaline seems to really bring us back to the body and its emotions and realities.

I'd say for therapeutic doses, somewhere around 300–600mg is where the rubber really hits the road. Mescaline doesn't tend to be TOO transpersonal or visionary, even at higher dosages. It does tend to bring people into their body, mind, emotions, and psyche.

Most of the research chemicals are mescaline derivatives or, more technically, derived from phenethylamine, from 2-CB to DOI to 2C-T-7. I have had many forays into working with these research chemicals and feel that 2-CB is perhaps the most useful one. But I stopped taking all synthetic phenethylamines many years ago, as I found them too rough and potentially damaging to elements of the human body that are not presently understood. Anyone can feel a bit seedy the day after taking these chemicals. I came to the conclusion that it was best to just stick with mescaline, even though sourcing and preparation can be annoying at times. Purely synthetic mescaline, I have found to be largely a waste of time—just empty and without spirit or soul.

If I was to initiate a complete newbie with psychedelics, I would probably start them with mescaline, as it is so stabilizing and easy to navigate. Many people have expectations that mescaline is going to be some kind of crazy journey—and for sure, it can be at very high dosages, which is going to take a lot of cactus. But the advantages of mescaline are its clarity, stability, and friendliness. So much so that people taking it for the first time might feel a bit more underwhelmed than they might expect.

Ketamine is probably the second psychedelic I would give to people who are new to this space, though I am not sure ketamine is hugely therapeutic. I had one client who wanted to take ketamine IM and then smoke DMT on top of that, just to break through the steel cage of his own mind, and that worked to some degree. But honestly, I just don't find Ketamine useful with most people. Sure, it can interrupt depression and have some therapeutic benefits, but not quite in the same way that the classical psychedelics have.

When it comes to iboga, the full-flood doses are something that are quite specialized in terms of what people require in terms of facilitation. When giving people these "flood" doses of 15–30 grams of root bark, you really do need to have experience with these dosages and have a good connection to the plant. I know people who confidently give high-dose iboga regularly, never with any serious issues, yet they also truly know what they are doing. Again, everyone knows this space is fraught with potential issues.

I personally prefer working with the root bark and have not been attracted to taking purified ibogaine.

There is definitely something to be said for providing a bit of root bark as well when giving people the TA (the total alkaloid extract from the plant) or isolated ibogaine —just to bring them into contact with "the wood," which has its own magic.

Sy Tzu in South Africa developed the "stream dose," as opposed to a flood dose. That is a dose of 3–8 grams of root bark, which is much more accessible to people, which doesn't necessarily require all the heart and kidney tests, and people can recover quite quickly from—perhaps even to get up and drive within 38 hours. Whereas with a flood dose, people may only be able to drive on the 5th day after ingestion.

With these stream dose amounts, you can also give people iboga in small groups, and I have done a few iboga groups with this sort of dosage myself. As a facilitator, my understanding is that "Dr. Iboga" takes over quite easily and gives people what they need in the space.

The stream dose is, of course, still psychoactive, just not as visual or potentially immersive as "flood" doses. Even one or two grams of iboga can still be quite psychoactive. People can still receive insights and healing with this dose, and the experience is more equivalent to a 2 or 3 gram psilocybin mushroom experience.

The flood dose for many people might be a once-in-a-lifetime experience, or something that people only do very rarely in their lives. For one thing the time investment is quite immense. The "stream" dose is more accessible and something that people can reach for regularly when they feel they need a "tune-up."

For people who are not addicts and are seeking clarity

and resolution of personal issues, I recommend they start with 1 gram of iboga root bark, then go to between three and 5 grams. I believe people should think about taking higher "flood" doses after first making friends with the plant. I'm personally not convinced that taking voacangine derived isolated ibogaine is the best way for people to experience this space, especially in a hospital bed in Mexico with all the staff, IV injections and potential distractions.

That is not to doubt that these experiences can truly work for many people, I just believe it is better to experience this space in a more organic, and less controlled, less medical environment, perhaps not at such a high price point. Very experienced facilitators of iboga know that if they do everything correctly, there is almost no risk. The highest risk with ibogaine mostly arises with people who are in poor health and who are drug addicts.

Chapter 7

Preparation and Integration

In terms of screening clients, I might have a different approach from many people. I believe that everyone can partake of most psychoactive medicines, as long as you get the substance and dose right. If your work is effective —careful, considered, and customized—then you can cater to each person, as psychoactive medicine should be helpful to most everyone, even if the dosage might be relatively small.

There are many healing practitioners of all kinds who carry out sincere and powerful sessions over 1-2 hours as spiritual healers, bodyworkers, and therapists of various kinds. They will not generally be "screening" people out (as pretty much anyone can come to them) but they sometimes will aim to reduce the potency of what they do, so there is not TOO MUCH potentially highly confronting processing work for the individual, especially if they are new clients. Similarly, I think anyone can do half to one gram of mushrooms and get something out of it, but not everyone is ready for the confrontation of five or more dried grams.

Many people may not be prepared for the fallout of a

true red pill experience, especially if such a person is not engaged in conscious self-work. The medicine may cause them to be catalyzed into a space where they may not feel they are ready to do this type of self-work. They may not even have any conception of what self-reflective inner work is, perhaps largely being enmeshed in "normal" cultural forms of hedonism and self-interest. Yes, some people have a profound and immediate awakening when they realize they are part of the earth, or understand that they are deeply connected to the cosmos, but the existential work involved in the fallout from these big cosmic experiences can be overwhelming, destabilizing and very time consuming for many.

People generally know when they are ready, and often they are more ready than they think they are by the time they approach a practitioner. Practitioners of various kinds often provide intake forms, whereby clients give information about their diet, stresses, life habits, health, injuries, what they want out of the session, trauma, drugs (legal or illegal), and this kind of PDF form can be easily sent and it is relatively easy for clients to fill out.

That is fine, but with this work, I also believe verbal communication of 30–60 minutes is really necessary before deep work with a client. I ended up in the last few years of my work with ayahuasca groups, wanting to do this Zoom call with every single person I worked with, and I found a deeper familiarity with what is actually happening for my clients, enabled a much better all-round experience and result for them.

I will generally hold an initial 30 to 60 minute Zoom

or phone call, whereby I can use intuition to really zero in on what is happening with the client. A combination of conversation and gut feelings is always going to be where you can zero in on many of the root causes of someone's troubles. But then again, there are many layers and levels in a human being. Often only through working with people over a longer period of time are you going to find out levels of trauma and their core issues, which may be repressed or hidden.

Sometimes I will not work with people based upon their initial communications to me; sometimes it might just be a feeling or a sense that the person isn't ready or is a mismatch. However, this is rarer than you might think, as people generally know what is a match for them. What some people might need are other supportive modalities and processes, and not to engage in psychoactive processes that bring up all their issues, often all at the same time. Such people may just need processes that allow them to slowly unpack what they need to work on.

We must remember that there are many modalities that are powerful and effective for people who want to address trauma and deeply rooted issues in the body and mind. What clients tell me that work the best for them are modalities such as Internal Family Systems, somatic psychotherapy, various forms of bodywork such as network chiropractic and its various offshoots, family constellation, and any number of processes and methods that are effective and supportive for the individual. But also, it appears to me that it is more the quality of the therapist that is most important and not necessarily the modality itself. We also shouldn't discount talking therapy in and of itself, and some people may not truly progress when taking psychedelics unless they are supported with some form of therapy.

In terms of the actual process of screening people, much of it will depend on what you present to the public as your "shopfront." My reputation has always been to give people the stronger doses, not to buy into often pseudo-traditional mumbo jumbo, and not to appeal to "spiritual" visual signifiers or assume some kind of trendy identity that appeals to the masses. I also tend to say a lot of unpopular, non-obvious controversial things on social media. So I have already set myself up to screen out a LOT of people. And because I have been in the media and on podcasts fairly often, my approach was always to deter the wrong sorts of people from coming along to my events.

People would always be surprised that dickheads, drones, drongos and dropkicks (my blunt language also tends to discourage the problematic types who are commonly "easily offended") would not be present—that's because I would have already "offended" them. They just wouldn't want to come. And of course, the issue would never be with THEM; it would always be with ME (in their eyes). In some sense, you've got to accept and see that a lot of the rumor mills and gossip can work in your favor, even though a lot of it can be distorted and just straight up containing no truth at all. The kind of people who glibly believe feeble and shallow gossip, are also likely not the kind of people you want to work with anyway.

However, if I were just trying to market to the lowest

common denominator (which is what most marketing IS, as the great unwashed are the largest audience) and appeal to the man on the street, my clients would be the typical man on the street and all the problems he brings.

I have had a situation where my friends were organizing a Graham Hancock talk in Cape Town, South Africa, and the esteemed Mr. G.H. told people in the audience that if they were interested in drinking ayahuasca, to talk to my friends Nash and Nisha.

I then ran 2 consecutive weekends of Ayahuasca drinking with Graham Hancock fans, who are not exactly mainstream people. Suddenly, I had all these inquiries from people taking 3 different types of pharmaceutical medications at the same time, when it was very rare for me to get even one inquiry like this. These 2 weekends were deeply challenging for me. I don't have anything against accountants, but one night, 3 accountants attended. The issue was with the attitude of the people; some of them were thoughtful and interesting, but there was an undertone that was not serious—just curious, not truly prepared or wanting real change. None of them talked to each other when they arrived; they were just in silence, which was very unusual in my normal groups. I felt these people were not in any way committed to awakening or waking up. In common terms, most of them had lived their lives serving mammon more than anything else. The vibe was brittle and unforgivingly sharp, reflecting the predatory and self-serving nature of Cape Town, one of the last holdouts of old school colonialism in the world if you ask me (despite being a pretty harbourside city).

There were energies the group had brought into the space that did not want to move. At one point, I saw gray aliens and then blacked out for a time. I couldn't steer this ship or get through to the participants. They were already sternly moving in the wrong direction. There was a woman whose blood pressure was extremely low—at one point, a helper and I had to hold her hand, as she said some beings told her it was okay if she departed this reality. I told her, "Please, not on my watch," and so myself and my helpers and I had to hold her hand and keep her in her body most of the night. I had to ask Nash and Nisha to chant esoteric Sanskrit mantras to break up spells and dark magic (which were also very evident), and finally, we were able to move this energy just a little. These 4 sessions over 2 weekends were some of the most challenging sessions I have ever done, with all kinds of characters, including a 75-year-old man who had to go into another room and cry, and also some beautiful, sincere people who connected with the plants in a unique way. The next year, I held another weekend group in Cape Town, and this time it was only filled with my usual crew of sincere explorers who wanted to go deep, and that went a lot smoother.

As psychedelics become increasingly popular, many of us working in this space have had to tighten up and be aware that many people may not have the same sincerity or real foundation to take advantage of this work, as we have previously been used to over the years. With medicalization, comes people believing they can just take a psychedelic pill which will fix their problems, when this is just not the case. Psychedelics are potent because they have the potential to create real change, but if people are brittle and resistant to fundamental personal transformation, their effect will be blunted.

And of course, many people are in dire straits, in a fix, in patterns which they are trying to change or they are addicted to illegal or legal drugs. I know some facilitators who are just not interested in filling up the holes in damaged people, who are increasingly coming their way, but are more interested in helping people to wake up to their true nature and evolve in consciousness and the becoming of humanity, which is usually much more inspiring.

This has always been the case with iboga providers I've talked to over the years, who generally prefer to work with people ready to truly heal rather than opiate addicts, who are typically just seeking to "get off the gear." Working with heroin addicts and addicts in general, who are often in a very difficult and unhealthy place, can be quite dispiriting, especially when relapses are so common. It is generally more inspiring and encouraging to work with people who are already on top of their lives, who are ready to work on themselves and become healthier and more aligned people. There is a feeling that with such people, we are bringing more light and alignment to humanity, rather than just bringing people back from the abyss.

We can never underestimate how working with just one person can change the consciousness of many—and not just in the sense of morphic resonance, whereby what the individual changes in themselves affects humanity in general. In this sense, our interactions with others can cause chain reactions that are difficult to track and can be mind-expanding to think about. I have felt at times that much of the deep processing after a group weekend implies that timelines have been changed for the better—not just in the immediate future but in the distant future, and surely in other realities and dimensions as well.

In terms of physical preparation, I tend not to emphasize this issue, especially related to diet. It is extremely easy for practitioners to send a list to clients telling them to eat only organic food and only certain kinds of food, and surely it is beneficial to get people to eat healthier food in the lead-up to a session. However, I prefer not to prescribe or assume I know what diet is best for individuals, and I don't believe that telling people to be disciplined with their diet for only a couple of weeks is going to make too much of a difference. I don't believe people should have the idea that there is a special or healthy way of eating. People already know—or should know—what is good for them in terms of food. When dealing with ayahuasca, there is much discussion about "the dieta," which is mostly related to drinking ayahuasca over a week or month, not just for a night or weekend. The dieta itself is a replica of an indigenous diet, with no salt, sugar, or oil. I personally found that the only truly serious health issues arise when people consume foods containing high amounts of tyramine, such as red wine and blue-vein cheese, ingested twenty-four hours before or after drinking ayahuasca.

I think back to a story I heard in South Africa about a couple of serious ayahuasca guys who followed the strict diet before drinking. They brought along their friend, who picked up some McDonald's on the way to the session, snorting cocaine in the car. Far from the medicine not working for him, this guy had an utterly vivid, transcendent experience—representing humanity at some sort of galactic court hearing, articulately speaking to the delegation as to why humanity should be given the provision to continue existing. Nevertheless, many people do eat a lot of junk food and I have seen more than a few people very much distracted by a physical level experience, where the toxicity of their own lifestyle of recreational drugs and junk food is being processed, and they might feel very nauseous and distracted.

Psychological preparation is so unique to each person and tends to happen automatically, just as integration can happen automatically. Yes, both processes can be optimized, but they often don't need to be. The basis for both preparation and integration, is having respect that strong processes either will occur or have occurred. Unfortunately, many are still enmeshed in a paradigm that is quite shallow and so they do not consider not just the psychological shifts, but the ontological changes in worldview that can easily happen in an experience that opens our eyes to levels of reality we might not have consciously perceived before.

We must remember what is obvious to us: that these compounds are optimizing and accelerating awareness in the human body and mind, toward a more expansive reality. This new ground—and awareness of new ground —can be very intimidating, but also very inspiring. This can often lead us to question the ground upon which Western human beings are living. Generally, First World people are very much stuck in their heads, in problem-solving consciousness, which is quite restrictive. Psychedelics can give people the ability to see what is outside the mind—that which has not yet been mapped or perhaps even understood by the frameworks of the time. This immersion into the mystery should be inspiring and lead us to more deeply question and see what we don't understand and attempt to understand what we can. Of course, this process can be challenging and can consist of most of what integration is for many people.

Psychedelics give the Western mind the ability to process emotions more easily, make more contact with their soul, and to embrace that the mind and ego are not the way, and begin aligning with the soul's purpose and the soul's direction. Issues like depression can evaporate, as depression often appears to be something like the soul's way of telling the organism that it is feeling stuck. When people's soul and purpose align into a space of dreaming awake, they experience a lightness and fresh data, clearing the heaviness of depression—which, in many respects, is also blocked human potential—appearing to occur when the soul is not moving in the way that it wants to move in this reality.

Chapter 8

Group Cactus and MDMA Weekend

The future of psychedelic therapy is largely not in one-on-one sessions, but in groups. These groups are effective because they allow each person to engage with the medicine within an overall container provided by the facilitator, which allows a more realistic healing environment where other human beings can provide support and feedback apart from the facilitator. Plus, it is not cost efficient to give one-on-one psychedelics for the many sessions it may take for people to gain healing. Perhaps a better model we will likely see more of in the future, is one in which spaces and containers are created for people in which to self direct and engage with the environment and each other.

What I could clearly see running my ayahuasca weekends, and also on longer retreats (which lasted 10–12 days), was that the social healing that people experienced through connections and community was just as potent as the medicine itself. Even in one weekend whole new friendship circles would form. The quality of people who attended these weekends was generally very high, and many people would have issues finding such people of like mind in their day to day lives.

What would astound me was how different types of people would come in waves of different groups of people—one weekend it was mostly all rough, tatted-up guys riding motorbikes, and then the next weekend it was all inner-city, latte-sipping artistes and refined ladies. Another weekend, it was all space-case headcase space-cadets, and the next weekend, completely grounded people in their bodies and smooth operators. So there appeared to be something IN people that brought them to come together in these weekends, and I saw that this coming together is perhaps underestimated as a way that people could gain hope in other human beings, and see themselves in other people.

I carried out many cactus walks in Australia since 2013 (mostly for free or by donation), where we would all take cactus on a Sunday and go walking over 10-20 kilometers. This chance to connect with nature and each other I saw was quite precious—to make new connections with high-quality people. And I perceived that bringing people together was a very important role. I first learned about these cactus walks in South Africa, and there are people there whom I met who religiously take cactus and walk in nature together every Sunday. These cactus walks I held really took off, especially around Melbourne with 20 or more people commonly attending, but I did them in Sydney and Brisbane as well. Some years later, I began charging money for them.

I felt that there was something vital about being in the

tribe, this herd, and good conversations could flow in that group space. There was often lots of laughter and a feeling of belonging, which I could see was missing in most people's lives. So many people were alienated and felt divorced and disparaged about the overall state of the human race. But the cactus walks provided a strong filter—as the only people who would show up were those who were adventurous enough to take psychedelics in nature with strangers. This meant that the quality of people who came along was very high. Then people were able to feel that others were actually okay, and consequently, that they were okay too. Then there began to be a sense of trust emerging, and an awareness of one's issues coming up and being processed in this space with other people who were mostly on the same page as you.

The format of MDMA and cactus weekends came about after one ayahuasca weekend in 2017, where some attendees, my helpers, and others who had previously come on retreats with me, decided to rent a cabin in the forest on a beautiful property for a few days in country NSW and take cactus and MDMA. It turned out to be a magical weekend, connecting with this beautiful nature and having great conversations, and so I thought to create it as an event that I would invite the general public to.

For a few years, I did these events perhaps two or three times a year. They were never THAT popular, but it was always the right number of people, between 8 to 12 people most times. I would book a beautiful house in nature for Friday, Saturday, and Sunday night. People would arrive on Friday night when they could, as many were working, and sometimes the location might be 3 hours from where they lived in the city. Oftentimes, people would fly in from regional areas or from other cities. Generally, I would hire a cook and helper to make dinner for everyone on Friday, or perhaps I would cook something myself, like dosas or pasta.

Initially, there is often a bit of awkwardness between participants, and I always find a lot of negative projection in any group setting when people first meet, with some elements of distrust and awkwardness. After a couple of hours, I find this distrustful projection falls away, which is why I find it is important for people to just get to know one another on the first night without any other agenda. People usually have their own room or share a room with someone else, or if they are a couple, they will normally have a room to themselves.

The big question for me when beginning these events was, do we do MDMA first or cactus first on the Saturday? The answer was that both scenarios worked. Sometimes the closeness created by doing MDMA on Saturday allowed the Sunday cactus walk to be more coherent. However, taking the cactus on the Saturday also opened people up to getting to know one another, and then by having the MDMA on Sunday, they could go deeper into trusting the other people. This might mean talking to other participants about what was really going on in their lives and being somewhat vulnerable.

For the cactus walk, a walk of 10–15 kilometers, I find optimal. Then people can stop, sit, and just enjoy nature. I have done walks of 20 kilometers, but that can be quite taxing, and some people may lag behind. Especially at higher doses, the shorter walks are better. After all, it is about nature more than it is about the walk, per se. The walk is great too, but just sitting in nature is a good time to stop and reflect without devices or agendas.

On Sunday morning, generally we'll have breakfast around 9 a.m., and then around 1 p.m. or so, take the MDMA together. For the MDMA, I will give each person a different dose—normally from 100 to 150 mg —and with some people I'll give them up to 200 mg.

What happens when people take MDMA together in a group is that magic happens—walls fall away, suddenly touch becomes easy and communication becomes effortless. I once had a middle aged Croatian man attend who was very quiet when he arrived, fairly stoic and silent, and then when he took the MDMA he just opened up and began talking. We couldn't get him to stop, and yet what he was saying was so interesting. After that, he opened up a lot in his life in general and appeared to become a different person socially.

People will generally organize themselves into spaces where it suits them. Some people will sit by themselves. Some people will talk. Couples may interact. People will tend to fall into one another and into close proximity and touch. Sometimes the whole group will self organize into their own play and games. People who are used to taking MDMA at clubs and raves are amazed at how different this space is, because you are giving the MDMA state real space to be present, whereas dancing on it can be perceived as kind of a waste of time, because the effects are then only as a kind of glorified amphetamine.

What we are doing here is creating our own party. But I don't play music for much of this, just give people space. Because MDMA is generally not sexual in nature, I've not found any sexualization occurring in this space—but for sure, it could. The purpose of this space is to feel a sense of trust and safety in a group setting. The purpose of it isn't to address trauma, and there is no space given in these groups for therapy. What is happening is that people find a space of naturally being useful to one another and provide each other with the input and communication that they may find useful. For example, one young man from Singapore who once attended a weekend, had this experience of being accepted for being gay, when in his culture he had never felt that before.

But also, the idea is to create a good time with other human beings—to create good memories, to truly feel like you're living. I've had many people tell me this was the "best weekend ever." It is also a time we can, in a way, be registered and taken into account, and brought to exist in other people's awareness, lives, and memories. In many respects, to be human, we must be witnessed by other human beings. Many people in our society are disenfranchised and burnt out by other people, often understandably so. Even if you think it is 99% of the people doing the burning, there is still the 1% of the population who are worth being concerned with and worth connecting with.

People are seemingly increasingly alienated—looking

at a screen and knowing that this is not the way we are nurtured and given spiritual nutrition. Yes, we can receive spiritual nutrition and love from ourselves, but we are wired evolutionarily to be in small hunter-gatherer tribes. To come back to this feeling of a small tribal group I have found is very important. In the course of human history, lone-wolf human hunter-gatherers would have been the exception rather than the rule. In a survival sense, we need each other, but we also need each other in an existential, spiritual sense. Modern society often appears opposed to the values of community, and it appears difficult for modern people to give up their selfishness, needs, and wants, to come back to thinking about the tribe and group, rather than only about themselves.

There is also an element in group work whereby I have seen difficult trauma resolved through group sharing, that has not shifted by sharing with friends or psychotherapists one-on-one. There is something potent about the whole tribe hearing and facing the assessment and judgment of the tribe. In one of my 10-day retreats, I had a man in his late fifties tell us at the beginning of the retreat that he could talk about an incident that happened when he was younger that left him traumatized—but he was unable to tell the group, only to communicate this to individual people.

The incident happened when he was an assassin for a well-known three-letter spy agency. He was a brilliant young man, chosen by the organization to take out terrorists and killers. He knew these people tortured and killed many, and that he was helping to take out these ultra-violent people was not an issue for him. But then one day, he accidentally killed an innocent bystander, and this absolutely shook him. He talked about it to his superiors, and they shrugged it off and didn't give him any assistance to process this incident psychologically. He felt betrayed and had to leave his deployment and spent the next couple of decades away from civilization, carrying a vast guilt he couldn't overcome—far away in distant lands, on oil rigs or ships out in the middle of the ocean.

Eventually, after drinking ayahuasca a few times on the retreat, he came to feel free to share his story with the group and get it off his chest. Then suddenly, the guilt he'd carried for decades vanished, and he felt forgiven and accepted by the community at large. I've seen this in sharing circles where people have viscerally brought forward their white-knuckled, shaking fear and trauma—in which they became more free from sharing it in a group setting. These debriefs I have found to be very powerful. People have said they are unable to share with their friends and family as they do in such debriefs. I have found it common that people will cry in these debriefs, too. I have commonly had circles of 15 to 20 people, where at least a third of the group are crying. There is definitely an element of people needing to confess. It might even just be for not being a good enough dad, for example. When people can be vulnerable, other people can resonate with what they are saying.

Sometimes it might be disappointing that people don't share that much. Many people feel burnt, or when they previously have shared in this manner, that information has been used against them later, which can feel like a big betrayal and letdown. If we are dealing with a temporary group, this factor is largely taken out of the equation. Yet even with "strangers," not everyone feels free to share.

On the other hand, oversharing might not be good either. I had one man admit he was a pedophile in a group sharing and explain his struggle and his attempt to heal from the sexual abuse he experienced as a child. This might be taking it too far, as then you have a whole bunch of people feeling concerned about the safety of children and whether they should warn the authorities. Indeed, this man had tried to share his plight with psychologists and friends, often getting dropped by friends and having psychologists alert the authorities, leading him to be suicidal at times.

This does make us think that the Christian practice of confession is something that is perhaps psychologically useful. Perhaps one of the most valuable things we can take away from Christianity, is the emphasis on mercy and forgiveness. But can we just forgive all these priests taking sexual advantage of young boys, for example? Is this the right way to approach the issue? Certainly, violence or vengeance isn't going to resolve the issue either, if we truly want to bring about healing for such people.

What about these soldiers in warfare who shoot children in the head or slaughter innocent civilians willingly, but are left with CPTSD, which never goes away? This sort of thing has been happening for a very long time. "The devil made me do it" isn't really a valid defense, even in Christian paradigms. But it is clear to see that many of the actions of the guilty may have been instigated by forces that compel them to perform wrong actions, and not everyone is strong enough to resist these forces. Such people, too, need to be forgiven by a community in order to move on with their lives, not just by the faceless, bloodless priest in the corner.

Chapter 9

Smoking Tryptamines

I personally think there is often far too much emphasis on the smoking of 5-MeO-DMT in the global milieu. 5-MeO-DMT can provide people with a sense at having arrived at higher spiritual states, when these are largely a priori states of being. With 5-MeO-DMT people can realize mystical states of samadhi and union with the divine, but once you've experienced that, it really is time to hang up the phone.

Unity is quite easy actually, and 5-MeO-DMT can take us to unity. Whereas N,N-DMT (or regular DMT) tends to take us more into duality. Both molecules are doorways into their own truth, but neither can show us the entire truth. The truth of reality is much more complex and paradoxical than brain states of cosmic unity or duality can reveal.

I have never really worked much with 5-MeO-DMT or the venom from the *Bufo alvarius* toad which contains 5-MeO-DMT. Facilitating 5-MeO-DMT can require a lot of careful support, due to the extreme reactions people can have to it and people may scream, make a lot of bodily movements, experience extreme emotional states or even try to run away.

I believe there is much therapeutic value in smoking low doses of pure 5-MeO-DMT (say around 5mg), but I don't like the harshness and forced nature of synthetic 5-MeO-DMT. I have been carrying out a lot of research on plants which contain natural 5-MeO-DMT and discovered one plant in Asia called *Phyllodium pulchellum* which contains DMT, 5-MeO-DMT and beta-carbolines, which when taken as a tea, can give low dose 5-MeO-DMT experiences. See the article on my web site "Why Phyllodium Pulchellum is the Best Candidate for the Vedic Soma".

https://julianpalmerism.com/phyllodium-soma/

Even though for sure there can be intense cathartic and healing processes that do occur with 5-MeO-DMT, some people can also react poorly to the experience and do not necessarily find it beneficial, something I've not observed as much with DMT.

I do think the "breakthrough" DMT experience is worthwhile for people to experience at least once or perhaps a few times. Although I would recommend to people more the sub-breakthrough DMT experience which changa provides as a more sustainable path for smoking DMT. And it is truly worth smoking DMT, because the visuals, the states and experiences are going to be a few levels deeper and crisper than the states you can get to by taking DMT orally, say, in the form of ayahuasca.

I largely only work with changa these days and not

crystal DMT, as I realized people would have better recall and integration with changa because of the ayahuasca vine. Changa (20 to 50% DMT infused into herbs including ayahuasca) can be a profound therapeutic tool and many people around the world these days are holding changa groups and carrying out one on one work with changa. This medicine can open people up immediately to an interconnected and meaningful reality, which often gives people a felt sense of hope. Within minutes people's systems can be reset, their pineal blasted open (in the best possible sense) and they can receive guidance and data that can help them to align with their soul. If anything, I think the smokeable tryptamines in general are most useful for cracking western people out of their "pseudo-rational" minds, into a vaster reality beyond ideologies of materialistic nihilism.

Because I came up with changa in the early to mid 2000's, people might think that I still work with it a lot, yet that is not the case. Yes, I have given DMT and changa to hundreds of people and have held quite a few changa groups, but there are many people who have worked more with changa than me and I am merely a changa pioneer. I've held changa groups here and there, but it has never been a consistent practice of mine. In the 2000's I held impromptu changa circles in places as diverse as Siberia, Bosnia, Spain, Syria, South Africa, Mumbai, Peru and the hills around Nimbin.

I believe one of the best ways to smoke changa in a group is to organize people in a circle and pass around a joint as people inhale and hold a puff or two, and then pass it around. The experience can be as gentle or as deep as people like it to be. This can be a social experience and people can go into the depths together in silence.

Probably the most important thing you need to take into account with DMT is how tricky it can be to smoke, as it can be quite harsh on the throat and lungs. Some people are using vaporizers these days, which do work very well to enable people to smoke changa more easily. I have a friend who takes groups on a yacht and gives them all a big plastic bag to inhale, which contains changa smoke from a volcano vaporizer. First they experience the changa with their eyes closed and then in a later session with eyes open to appreciate the natural world.

But also a bong or "bubbler," which filters the thick smoke through water, is of course very effective too, and is my preferred method. For therapeutic purposes, some people these days are also pre-dosing their clients with Syrian rue so that the experience often lasts around 30 to 40 minutes, or people are giving successive doses of changa with a high MAOI content, so that the experiences last 30 to 60 minutes.

Much of the changa made these days contains a very strong MAOI imprint, which to my mind is not necessary, as many of the people making it don't truly understand the impact of smoked harmaline or harmine on the individual. This means the experience may be more heavy, grounded and emotional than it needs to be. To my mind, the best changa is balanced in its DMT and harmine components, and gives you groundedness, but also enables you to touch the transcendent as well. Also I think there is a magic in smoking the caapi vine which contains harmine, and many people are using harmalas extracted from Syrian rue, which to my mind doesn't have the same magic when smoked and can result in an experience which is too heavy, similar to the weighty side effects from a very heavy caapi vine tea.

Before smoking DMT, people are naturally going to be very apprehensive. The fear that people have is completely natural and is a message telling us that what we are doing is something serious, and I think this nervousness helps to bring people to have an innate respect for these states.

People generally hold 2 to 3 rounds when holding a changa group or giving changa to a client one on one, sometimes giving people a 4th round if they want it. Because of the harmine content in the vine, each successive changa dose is going to be stronger and the 3rd round can even last for 30 to 60 minutes at times.

When smoking changa or DMT, you do need to create a space where people can sit up when inhaling the smoke and then they need to be able to easily lie back down in a comfortable place with their eyes closed. I generally prefer to work without music, and like to give people total silence and space to go into what they need to. I also like to give people time to come back, and I let them speak first, rather than interrupt anything people in the group may be going through.

The first dose might be what is often called a "handshake" dose, a relatively small dose where people can make friends with the experience. After people are complete with the first round, then you can really give people a bigger, more normal dose. That might be anywhere from 60-200mg of 40% changa. Some people might not feel the need to do a third round, but many people will want to go deeper and some might even want a 4th round.

I like to hold a debrief afterwards where people can talk about their experiences, but I know facilitators who don't do this also. The entire process is probably best held over around 3-5 hours to give people enough time to drink some tea together with the other participants, be comfortable in the space, talk about their experiences and then be ready to meet the world afterwards.

Because changa is so short in duration, people often work with it combined with other substances, at the end of ayahuasca or during cactus. I have felt it is really best to give changa its own time and space, and not just give people more data to work with, just because you can, as this can overload people and they can have negative reactions, which I have heard of occurring quite a few times. I have spoken to one facilitator who finds it most beneficial to give changa its own time and space, on the day after a psilocybin session, which makes a lot of sense to me.

Chapter 10

Anatomy of an MDMA session

MDMA therapy has become quite popular in recent years as more and more people understand this state can be used to help people to process PTSD and trauma. I am by no means an expert in this often quite specialized modality, but I thought I would share how I conduct an MDMA session. In recent years I have been asked by people to hold sessions for them and have developed something of a basic protocol, which I think works well.

I prefer to do these sessions in a neutral location such as an Airbnb with good privacy and a decent amount of space around it. I also like to have a female assistant and helper, with either men or women.

Upon arrival, I like to spend an hour or so in the space with the client, being comfortable and relaxed in the space, not feeling rushed, drinking tea, talking about relevant expectations and issues that the client wants to address.

The MDMA is generally dosed between 100mg and 160mg, most typically 120mg to 140mg, in a gel cap taken down with juice or water. Then it takes about 40-60 minutes for the MDMA to arrive properly in their system and then the client can just enjoy the space and be comfortable.

I will often play music during this time, of a style that the client prefers. They may want to sit down or lie down, but I prefer them just to be silent, to go within and experience the ease, as their defences fall away, and they go into the spaciousness and feelings that the MDMA brings. This quiet time can last for half an hour or an hour, depending on where your client is at and what they want from the session.

Then the real work begins. For myself, I like to talk to people in a spontaneous way in order to naturally build trust. Not everyone is going to go as deeply into processing their trauma or core issues as you may like at times. For me, this space is a time to practice healing in an active sense, to bring people to contemplate themselves in a space of more openness and depth than they may ordinarily be able to access. It is time for people to feel connected. It is a time for people to talk openly and get things off their chest. It is a time and space for people to explore and see their potential. It is a time for people to feel open and safe, for their nervous system to relax and for them to explore self love and active understanding of themselves.

If there is a particular traumatic event that people have, I would like them to retell their story and go through their thoughts and feelings about it, and sometimes I may gently pry or ask questions. And it is important to remember that some people have serious trauma that has been repeated continually from an early age, so then you are often best addressing the trauma in its somatic nature and help people to shake it out of their system, for example.

This is a time and space for the human organism to process and make peace with the past, to bring back lost parts of themselves and release any fear that they may have. In my work, the conversation is entirely intuitive and I find the nature of MDMA can allow people to lead the conversation and you may just need to gently steer them.

This more verbal aspect of the session may last from 60 to 90 minutes and is in many respects the meat of the session, where you are attempting to allow the individual to process and work through what is on their plate and what is on their mind. They may talk about previous relationships, their hopes and their dreams, their plans and fears. But for the most part, people will often want to talk through their trauma and issues they haven't previously been able to explore, often even with a trusted therapist.

In an ideal scenario, I like to have a helper who can do spiritual healing, so the client can have a time in which to be passive and allow this type of deep level healing to occur. This part of the session is where people can process and participate in their own healing, or be in a more silent space. This might occur over an hour or so.

When the client is over the peak, I like to do body-work with them and in this space of increased surrender and openness, I like to allow them to release deeply held tension in the body which I find happens more easily when under the influence of MDMA, just as people are able to more easily release mental tension when they have taken MDMA. In this space, I am often talking to them about what I am feeling and experiencing in their body and helping them to process any somatic issues which seem to want to move. I want to encourage the body to shake and let go here, as I feel that this is a truly primary way the body can release trauma. I will often assist people in letting go at times by guiding them to release their jaw, so that it vibrates by itself, which can happen more easily with MDMA, and I call this process "Feeching". (look up the word feeching on my youtube channel to see my videos about it) I may even spend 20 minutes trying to get people to release their jaw, but some people can go into this let go immediately without any prompting.

There are times during an MDMA session where I might do some torping to clear any interference around the client, or I have even gotten clients to do bio-energetic exercises to break up blocked energy in the body. I might also introduce self love exercises, where I lead the client through every age of their life and see themselves in their innocence and growth process, and prompt them to tell themselves that they love themselves. This will be much easier for people to do when they have taken MDMA than in their regular state.

I might also find limiting beliefs, and help people to release them until they do not have so much charge. For example, one of my clients felt crippled by shame. Some of the beliefs we released were "I release the belief that I am disgusting" or "I release the belief that I am always wrong" or "I release the belief that I am bad" or "I release the belief that sex is dirty and sinful". It might take even half a dozen or more for people to keep releasing the belief until they feel the charge around the belief has actually been released. The client can intuitively hunt for limiting beliefs that they feel have charge or you can also suggest some for them.

The good thing about an MDMA session to my mind (say, compared to a more immersive psychoactive like psilocybin), is that it really does allow you as a therapist to bring a creative state of mind to the session, and attune to the client and bring them the right stimulus, touch, techniques and conversation that can enable their healing.

After the bodywork, I will just let the client chill out again and process, maybe they want to talk, maybe they want to just relax, have a cup of tea, a little bit of food or continue to process other things. Then at a certain point, there is a debrief that will generally naturally happen once they are coming out of the state. Then they might want to go for a short walk and spend time alone in nature. I like to give a lot of time after the session and not just disappear, and be present, to gently support the client for at least an hour or two after they have come down from the MDMA.

Chapter 11

Difficulties

Psychedelics often simply allow a confrontation with REALITY itself that is shocking to many people. People in industrial society are often insulated from what REALITY is—the good, the bad, the horrifying, and the startlingly beautiful. In a way, as facilitators, we are a bit like shepherds who have seen the terrain and know what it is like to confront these states. It is not with our words that we can primarily guide people, but with our presence—with the understanding that we have been through this, and come out the other side OKAY, hopefully more aware and able to live a constructive life. For most people, it just takes time to process and understand what we really are as humans and how we can truly be. It can also take weeks or months to come back to our center, identify what we want to let go of, and how we can be with reality more rightly.

There are a lot of truly sick people out there, and a lot of them understandably keep their cards very close to their chest. We don't live in a society that is particularly forgiving to perpetrators, rather we valorize victims. It is often the perpetrators who have as much, if not more, trauma than the victims. If we are to reduce trauma in the world, it is also in healing perpetrators, not just by patching up "victims."

At times, people will tell you who they really are and what they have really done. At the heart of it, people need to forgive themselves and forgive others, let go of grudges, and come to terms with humanity on its own terms, without whitewashing or backwashing, or generally getting lost in the noise of the human mind in all of its often quite indulgent complexity. Humanity is generally all kinds of gray, and there is good in the bad and bad in the good. This can be confronting when you form a certain relationship with a client and they reveal to you what they have done. I have had two clients tell me they are pedophiles. Both times I decided to continue working with them. One of them had a massive healing and completely reformed himself, and the other one—he appeared committed to healing and said he was not in any way active in the community. Then I realized there was a signature, and I wondered how many clients I had that were actually pedophiles, but hadn't revealed this to me. Seeing as I have worked with thousands of people, I assumed it must be around a dozen or two and that realization was very sobering.

If you are working with people closely, there are times when they will lash out at you and get violent. I have been bitten on the arm very badly. I have a few permanent scars on my arms from human nails, which drew a lot of blood at the time. I've had a big Russian guy threaten to smash my head in with a huge black Maglite torch after he had an "insight" that I was a pedophile! Luckily, his "boss" was present who was able to talk him down. I've had people leave the group space entirely, get in a taxi, and go home. I've had to take the car keys away from people while being verbally abused and threatened. I've had people run into the mountains and disappear into the forest, who later came back. I had one guy go out to urinate and then spend all night outside, break into other people's houses on a very cold night, and drink their wine. One time I had a woman scream so badly that the police were called by neighbors, and then the police and ambulance arrived to find the same woman unconscious. I simply told the police the truth and they eventually departed on friendly terms once they could see everyone was safe. One time, I had a participant try to have sex with another participant. A few times, I've had people lose it so badly that I've had to pin them down and have other people help me contain them as they scream and thrash around. There have been many times where I've been helping people in their shitty space of vomiting, where they have completely lost the plot, and I've had to help them back. Many times, I have been heavily exposed to people's traumas and sicknesses emanating from them, with people screaming out their bone chilling trauma. Obviously, much of this takes a toll, and you can find yourself wondering if you do really want to do this work.

Sometimes facilitation can appear easy and straightforward, and you are a bit like a pilot—taking off and landing on firm ground again, and often not doing THAT MUCH on autopilot in between. However, as the pilot, you are responsible for all the people in your care, and the degree to which they can trust you is the felt sense they have—that in an emergency, you will take the actions required to keep the plane in the air, or at least, as unscathed as possible. Some people I know who have begun to facilitate, might mistakenly come to feel quite confident, and then they might have a difficult session, and want to give up, saying that it's just too hard. It does appear that we are tested at times, and we might not always pass the test or act in the best way possible. We might not always say the right thing or may not always provide the most accurate direction or wisdom to our clients. However, we are not performing brain surgery here, where one wrong move is going to kill somebody. Yet, we are dealing with people in very fragile and suggestible states and we have a certain amount of power and responsibility to do right by them and not to misuse the power that we have. You can expect to be triggered and challenged in this work, and so the aim here is to attempt remain as centered as you can and not to react too much.

You can expect all kinds of difficulties and challenges to occur to if you choose to continue to work with often traumatized and potentially volatile people. There appears to be a certain point in carrying out this work when you might get a bit of a run of challenging experiences, one in which many people may want to give up facilitating. This is perhaps where the rubber hits the road for many facilitators, when you have to decide how you respond to people's difficult experiences and whether the difficulty and stress are really worth it for you.

I don't know of any way to bring people down from

a state where they go into a space of total insanity, where people may be screaming or going into repetitive loops, perhaps saying the same kind of thing over and over. I have found that tuning forks placed over the thymus work to some degree, but I've mostly found you just have to keep the person physically safe and let them go through it, until they naturally come out of it.

Oftentimes, there appears to be some deep processing going on in these chaotic states—a kind of letting go where the individual is just allowing their full expressive self come to the fore, even though it might be noisy or not make much sense. Sometimes these experiences can be like a purge of psychosis. However, for the individual going through these experiences, afterward, they can have a deep sense of shame or guilt about exposing those undignified parts of themselves, and also for potentially interrupting others. I've only ever heard of one facilitator in the world who is said to be able to truly bring people out of these spaces, but I also question whether people need to be brought out of these states. Perhaps they need to go this deep inside themselves, even though they might be caught up in a loop.

Although there are many potential issues involving their clients, the main battle I have found is within. What I continually see is facilitators getting a big head when people give them a lot of praise. They accept the praise and begin to think that they are ALL THAT. It can be tricky when you have not just one, but potentially dozens of people praising you, wanting to elevate you, and experiencing their positive projections and transferences cast onto you. Most people are susceptible to becoming someone—a SHAMAN or worker of magic, a maestro, or the one who has the power in the space. This power can easily get to people's heads, and we all know what they say about power. And yet, nothing in this work should be about power, and we shouldn't perpetuate the idea that power has anything to do with this work.

We need to come back to being servants of the people, rather than feeling a need to have any kind of dominion over them. We shouldn't be trying to control them or getting any lame kicks from telling them what to do. We need to be secure enough in ourselves to be able to empower other people. Attention, in my opinion, should not be drawn to us too much, and we need to continually come back to being servants of our clients—not in a servile way, but in the understanding that they are paying good money for us to bring quality attention and careful consideration toward them.

In this role, we don't really have the right to interfere with people's lives as if we are the big schoolteacher who is trying to teach people a lesson. Perhaps the way we need to go about things is how the plant teachers regard us—they are trying to help us, but they don't interfere in our choices. We are not just being exposed to people's vulnerabilities, but often their difficulties, issues, and traumas, which can be deeply triggering and perhaps at times quite relevant to where we are. You need to not emotionally react in an overt way and remain impartial in order to help people, and there is obviously such a thing as client confidentiality.

Working with people is challenging, as people have their own direction and orientation. It isn't up to us to change people, even if it were possible that we could change them at all. In many respects, it is through how we operate and our level of gentility whereby we can inspire change. We will often not even know how we are positively affecting people. But at the very least, we should have some means by which to look into our own blind spots and get some feedback from others. Though it is not always easy to get good-quality feedback either.

Perhaps many people carrying out this work are just not up to the challenge of being at the standard that is truly required. Too often, people in this work get captured by entities that work through them, or they get seduced by their ego, or the power and its apparent trappings—or all of the above.

When I was in Colombia, I drank ayahuasca with a *curandero* who said he didn't want to have a bigger audience and become corrupted like all his friends who had become "rock star" shamans—seduced by the same old trifecta of sex, money, and power. Yes, some of these people are great medicine workers, but at the end of the day, I see us as all "chai wallas" or "divine bartenders."

When I first drank ayahuasca in Peru in 2005, I was struck by what a "guided experience" it often was. I felt like I was going through a car wash, where many energies were being moved FOR ME. And at the end, I often came out of the car wash feeling only superficially clean.

So much of the time, the shaman or curandero is trying to prove what magic they can provide in a psychic sense. But if you are truly secure in serving medicine, you don't need to prove anything to anyone or to yourself. I know that if you give me a person for a 3 or 4-hour session of healing without medicine, I can affect as much or even MORE change and healing than the plants can provide to people. This gives a certain security in just letting the plants do what they do and to try not to interfere too much in that process.

Another thing you can commonly observe is people becoming reliant on the medicine space for their spiritual connection or sense of growth—perhaps becoming overly reliant. A lot of people need to stop taking any kind of medicine for a long period of time, whether that be months or even a year or two. Sometimes taking a lot of psychedelics can move a lot of frequencies through your system. People can become seriously ungrounded by all this top-heavy psychic phenomena, on the verge of actually going a bit crazy—if not actually mentally unstable.

That being said, I think some people do need to take a couple of years to passionately and truly explore this space and get their "sea legs." When I first started out exploring psychedelics seriously in 2000, I would take a psychoactive two or three times a week for two years, and I felt that was an initiation into this space. At that point, I was unemployed and homeless half of that time, camping on the beach, staying with friends, or staying in questionable accommodations. I was pretty much full-time processing and integrating what I was experiencing. I was also a bit unstable and quite mad at times, but often in a cute way, such as talking in poetry. The issue can be that the more we align with these other-dimensional spaces, the more out of sync we can be with the social milieu of people around us.

It is a fine line between getting the "flight time" in and dealing with the turbulence of profound forays into oneself and the transcendent. People within society often do a good job of appearing unruffled, but we'd be better off admitting how profoundly disturbing it is to witness and perceive reality as it is, and how different the revealed reality is from the cultural reality we were indoctrinated into and taught was true when growing up.

Like so many things in life, facilitation is more about what you don't do, than what you do. Not needing to do anything can be mitigated by maintaining a stable presence and giving people assurance and a feeling of safety. If you are working with groups, you are often dealing with group politics, which can tend to escalate in longer retreats. In this space, you need to be diplomatic and not be too quick to take sides and inflame or exaggerate human situations.

Human beings can sometimes get bogged down in shallow, egoic indicators and petty circumstances. As I see it, our job is to keep our eyes on the horizon and keep us all moving forward together. Sometimes you will fuck up, too. We have to wear our inevitable mistakes and attacks from armchair critics who generally don't risk doing anything effective in the world. Sometimes you've got to roll with the punches. Within the bad, good can come too.

One time, I made a mistake and booked a property for the wrong dates. I arrived at the venue I had used before, a big house deep in the countryside, and we all set up and drank ayahuasca. Then a few families came through in three cars and told us they had booked the venue. I told them to go away, as that would not be possible, and said that they must have gotten the venue name confused with another, similarly named venue a bit down the road. 20 minutes later, I received a furious phone call from the old farmer who owned the house, saying I had actually booked for the next week and he told us to immediately leave the house for the 3 families.

The issue was that there was nowhere to go. It was an almost freezing night with a thick fog. It was 10 p.m. on a Friday night in the middle of nowhere, with the nearest town being a 40 minute drive away. I quickly made a decision about what to do and told everyone to just collect their things and go sit in their cars, without trying to panic or stress people out.

The medicine came in like a tornado, as people collected their things and went to their cars with their blankets. With a participant's help, I found a space outside to build a fire 100 meters away from the house. Eventually we made a great fire, and people began coming out of their cars as the deeply powerful medicine stabilized in its effect. The drama and stress had triggered people so much that the relaxation and release they felt when we were all safe and sitting around the fire was profound.

The next night, I hired a large and amazingly beautiful house and we all drank again inside the house, but it just wasn't the same heightened feeling and flow, and feeling of togetherness as we had experienced the night before. A couple of people thought I had deliberately created the situation as some sort of spiritual lesson in letting go.

Then there is the gossip, especially the "bad news post office" (or *Correio de más notícias* in Brazilian Portuguese) which is the spiritualized gossip identified within the Santo Daime church as a primary negative force in the world. This is the type of gossip, criticism, or negative information about others, which is communicated under the guise of concern, truth, or spiritual responsibility and this type of gossip is identified as a profoundly negative force within Brazilian Santo Daime church culture.

I found myself becoming a victim of this type of gossip very commonly, and sadly enough, a lot of it was clearly coming from other facilitators who were often the ones spreading the gossip. I realized many years ago that there wasn't anything I could do to stop people from talking negatively about me. Often the stories and gossip I heard about myself didn't have one element of truth in it at all. A lot of it was under the guise of concern or insight or wisdom, but was actually quite underhand. I also never found that any of these people who were spreading the gossip talked directly to me and shared their concerns or feedback in a framework of true care or healing.

Many of these stories that I heard back about myself were just so puerile and talked more of the psychological makeup of the people who created and shaped them via "Chinese whispers" than anything about me. I eventually realized that this kind of gossip often worked for me, in that it kept away the kind of people who believed that this sort of gossip represented any kind of truth at all.

In 2013, after I'd been holding ayahuasca groups for

11 years, I felt that at least the stories that people were telling about me never involved any kind of sexual misconduct or the usual stuff you would commonly hear about other men in this space.

In mid 2013, there was a woman in her late thirties who came to my group who did not appear to be in an entirely good way. I didn't know it at the time, but she was smoking meth to keep up with her ultra-high-performing corporate sales job. She was holding onto my arm during our intro talk, and she didn't seem quite stable. I knew she was interested in me as she had come around to my place once unannounced, just before I had to leave to another group, and she then seemed offended that I had to leave so quickly, which she later told me that she was.

During this group, she was dealing with the medicine fine though, and I thought to myself, "I wonder what would happen if I went over and kissed her during the group?" This is, of course, the kind of thinking that represents a slippery slope, and to be honest in hindsight, I'm not even sure these were my thoughts.

I thought at the time it would be an interesting experiment to see what would happen if I did this, so I went and kissed her—full-on French kissing and snuggled up with her for a few minutes a couple of times. It wasn't that everyone saw, but some people definitely noticed and were clearly not happy about it, going by the expressions they shared with me later.

Clearly none of this needed to happen. I suppose for me it was just an experiment to see how it would feel if I did this, as I'd always dealt with the inevitable female focus on me very well. And to make a move on a woman in a group, well that was unthinkable for me, not the least because it is completely unnecessary.

I guess it is one of those things where the word gets around, and so the obvious understanding I got out of it is that it is definitely not a good idea to kiss your client during a session! But at the very least, I felt what it was like to do that. Previously, I've never even cuddled with any clients—male or female.

We ended up having a short affair, which she was very keen on having. She was cheating on her husband and had been in an unhappy and sexless marriage for many years. In hindsight, I could see she was in a way using me as an excuse to break up with her husband, which is what ended up happening shortly after we got together. She thanked me for showing her love, and then, as quickly as she came into my world, she disappeared—only reappearing some years later, when I continued to interact with her as a friend.

In early 2021, I had a female client to whom I gave MDMA. I had wanted her boyfriend to be in the space, but he didn't want to be in the space with us, leaving me and her in a much more intimate space than I would have liked, where she began communicating her interest in me and she told me her boyfriend was not a real boyfriend, but more like a sugar daddy.

A few days later, she called me up and said she wanted to have sex with me. I told her that was off the cards, and she communicated she was saddened that I wasn't interested in pursuing anything with her.

Eventually, she came to a longer retreat in the

outback with her sugar daddy partner of 4 years. One night, when one of my helpers was facilitating and I was drinking, I had visions of having a child with her, which was very surprising to me.

I went over to help her for a few minutes as I normally would, as she would be struggling a lot when drinking ayahuasca. Before I left her, I gave her an almost involuntary peck of a kiss on the cheek—perhaps communicating a recognition of what I was seeing in the vision.

I went back to my space and felt psychic question marks coming from her direction. At the end of the night, I went over to her space, and she pulled me in for a cuddle, then told me her feelings for me and that I was the only man she felt safe with.

I didn't say much back to her and only stayed 20 minutes or so on her mattress, but her "boyfriend" saw us together. At 3 a.m., he confronted her. She told him she had feelings for me, which resulted in him leaving the remote retreat in his hired 4WD. "There goes my paycheck!" she said.

She did want to continue something with me and in our later conversations, the Eros became a living thing which didn't want to be denied; it was so strong and there was no way to turn away from it—a living force that demanded compliance. In fact, I felt to turn away from that wouldn't have been the right thing, which is also what I believe in hindsight.

Of course, this was something I struggled with a lot at the time and of course I knew that I was making my bed and lying in it. This woman's therapist perceived me as taking advantage of her, and I had a couple of remarkably clear psychic impressions that he was jealous, as I strongly intuited he was interested in her, and wanted to relate with her in some capacity, but he had to technically wait for some years before not working with her as a patient before that was possible.

I thought that there was some evolutionary potential in this connection, and I couldn't truly explain it at the time. But it turned out that I was right about this and perhaps, in a way, we did create a child.

Over some months we slowly traveled in the outback from Darwin through the middle of Australia, to Adelaide and then back to Melbourne. This woman had been in a cult for many years, and she was suffering from all kinds of mysterious pains and issues that had incapacitated her. She would wake up at 3–4 a.m., and I would begin to carry out torping clearing over her body, which are short sharp sounds that sound like a dog barking, to clear the entities attacking her. I kept up 1 to 2 hours of torping every morning for four months until she was finally free of many pains and impediments in her body. Being with her was how I learned to torp over people's bodies in my regular state. I should also say, she wasn't happy with any apparent power imbalance in our dynamic, and made it clear to me that she wanted to give as much healing to me as she received.

After five months, she was starting to feel good for the first time in her life. Even though the Eros was strong and many elements in our relating synced up well, I didn't desire to continue the relationship.

Fast forward to mid-2022, and perhaps the largest

current affairs TV program in Australia called *Four Corners* wanted to film a cactus walk, which they filmed south of Sydney. Then they later called me in for another interview in the ABC studio, making it sound like they just wanted to ask more questions.

The journalist then told me on camera that there had been reports of inappropriate sexual behavior to them. You could have blown me over with a feather. Of course I had been ambushed. How was I going to defend myself against the absurd, moralistic accusation of "inappropriate sexual behavior" when I didn't even know what that was? I don't think anyone watching knew what they were talking about either. The whole thing looked so embarrassing and cringey for the ABC. Yes, they had gotten their "gotcha" shots of me looking awkward, uncomfortable, and nervous, but most intelligent people could see they had betrayed me. To be honest, that was what made me feel most uncomfortable, alongside that, were the threats of possible legal consequences, which the journalist made clear in one of her leading questions, "Would you say that was a very large commercial quantity of illegal mescaline?"

The hyper earnest folks at the ABC had apparently been manipulated by my ex-lady friend to believe I don't know what. I certainly had no idea how I may have been "sexually inappropriate" in any way.

They also referenced a 5,000 word Facebook post I made in 2017 at the peak of #MeToo, analyzing the phenomena of #MeToo and how it could get absurd and blown far out of proportion by mobs of disgruntled people. This was related to an intimacy technique called mebbing (see mebbing.org), some early experiments with this technique in 2012-2013 naturally led to what I thought were consensual sexual relations and actually were! However, I underestimated the backlash and reputational attack from organized haters who sought to weaponize and castigate high-profile men who didn't "bend the knee" to their ideologies.

Now they were using that insightful post AGAINST me on national television. In real time, I knew anything I said would be edited out if it was meaningful, and anything I did say would be used against me in their editing.

In the interview, I brought up the incident where I had kissed a woman in 2013—somehow still in the space of wanting to help them make a good story—and yet most insightful viewers could clearly see how they also edited my retelling of the story. Interestingly, I was on the phone with that woman just before it aired, and she sensibly said what happened between us was nobody's business. After the piece aired on live television to about a million people, my father called me immediately and we just laughed: it was all just so absurd.

The fallout from this ABC story wasn't necessarily helpful or constructive in the Australian scene. Thinking people could see through it and I received many dozens of sympathetic emails from the general public. I held an ayahuasca weekend the next month in Victoria and almost all the participants were women. However, it is not particularly pleasant to be framed as something you are not, and for distrust and doubt to spread about you in the wider community.

In 2023, I was offered a potential gig on some kind of Celebrity Ayahuasca TV show, which I was curious about and when I mentioned this hit piece on the ABC, I was advised by a friend who moved among celebrity circles, that I needed to take legal action to clear my name. I decided to do so and eventually the ABC offered to settle the case out of court and issued a public statement where they said:

"On 25 July 2022 the ABC broadcast a Four Corners program titled "Psyched Up". The program included footage of a cactus walk with Julian Palmer and participants, as well as an interview with Mr Palmer during the walk. A second interview occurred in the ABC studio, where Mr Palmer was questioned about a Facebook post he made in 2017, and allegations of "inappropriate sexual behaviour" reported to the ABC. In the program Mr Palmer vehemently denied any wrongdoing. The ABC did not intend to suggest that the questions constituted anything other than inquiries into allegations and apologises if any viewers, including Mr Palmer, understood or inferred otherwise."

There is no moral to this story. In hindsight, I would have done exactly the same thing if I had to do it all again. If I were to be purely moralistic and ethical, and just close everything down, I would have missed the ideal opportunity, time, and place to learn torping with this woman. What we went through was a profound love affair that, I would say, worked for both of us at the time. She got the healing she wanted her whole life, opened up many new doors in her life and I learned a whole new modality of healing and experienced transformation and healing also.

However, clearly it was a highly distorted and vindictive narrative she was now pushing, later I heard from other people that she chose to communicate a black and white narrative whereby that I had kissed her, and seduced her, unfortunately ceasing to take any responsibility for her own decisions or actions. It was also clear to see now, she had sided back with her old therapist and "sugar daddy", both of whom clearly had an axe to grind.

Unfortunately, I've seen this sort of pattern repeated again many times from women who lie and gossip and attempt character assassination of men they have previously been in relationships with.

There is another facilitator I know who married a woman whom he met through his medicine work. When the relationship soured, she approached the media and police, claiming he was running a cult and abusing his power. Once again, she abnegated her choices, free will and claimed somehow he was brainwashing her into being with him. Unfortunately these kind of stories appear to represent a common toxic feminine trait, that our society hasn't appeared to come to terms with in any real sense.

Certainly, I'd say with the oncoming regulation of the more aboveground psychedelic facilitation space, there does need to be clear boundaries and frameworks that work so that there are clearly understood consequences. If the rules are too strict, people are going to break them, like they do in the regular therapy space. On the other hand, I think we can all see that to just leave the door open for potential sexual affairs and relationships is obviously not something that the community could get onboard with either.

Men who opportunistically take advantage of vulnerable women in this space is a real issue, obviously less of an issue is women who take advantage of men, although I have met a couple men who have been very much traumatized by highly inappropriate over-sexualized interactions with female facilitators.

If you are going to enter into a relationship with one of your clients and pay the inevitable price (whether that be now or later), you must ask yourself, "WHY?" Is this really love or lust? Is this truly a forever connection? You don't choose who you fall in love with, have a connection with, or who you feel you might have a mission with.

Perhaps in the future, there could be some kind of provision that is witnessed and supported by contemporaries, which would stop people from risking their license completely to be with a client, as we can commonly see in the medical and therapy space. Something like 3 to 10% of medical doctors around the world do report a sexual affair with a patient at some point in their career. Among therapists, this number is something like 3% to 8%. These are not insignificant numbers of therapists to whom these interactions are important enough to them, that they will risk their professional career to have these affairs.

If this is going to happen anyway in the psychedelic space, as it surely will and already does, then surely there could be a way for that occur that is witnessed and registered by the community at large, and remain within healthy, consensual boundaries and not mired in potential manipulation, abuse, fear, power imbalances and negative consequences.

Ethics is often the affair of abstracted armchair scholars who never do anything in the world. It can often be the case that you learn through your mistakes, and it is very easy to tell others what not to do. In reality, human beings do commonly break such rules, and love and lust are the most powerful forces that human beings contend with. What we are clearly seeing is that as this work becomes more overground and more mainstream, the rules and punishments for sexually engaging with clients will become more clearly defined, and perhaps just the strict enforcement of these rules is not entirely the most intelligent or humane way forward.

Talking to other facilitators in the underground, it is generally agreed that the people you work with are by far the most interesting people that you interact with in the world. Some of these people you meet may naturally become friends, and some of them may become lovers—not based on any power dynamics, but because of a real affinity or chemistry.

I've spoken with other facilitators about this, and these types of boundaries are something that many have struggled with at times. We all want to connect and be intimate, and these psychedelic spaces are some of the most intimate and human spaces that we can go into with others. But that doesn't mean that physical or sexual intimacy should in any way be a part of that. Human beings are often so complex, and the space of sexuality can often amplify this complexity—something that may not be helpful to those who are truly seeking healing.

Chapter 12

Entities

One of the main issues that psychedelic practitioners in the early 21st century will have to come to terms with is etheric parasitic entities. Their existence becomes very clear to almost everyone working with psychedelics long enough—say, for at least a decade or so.

We must understand that the primary defense of these entities is to remain hidden and unseen by human beings. You can meet very capable spiritual healers who have no particular insights into the influence of these entities. Such entities exist on a particular wavelength or bandwidth, which you must deliberately tune into and attune to.

Outright possession by these beings is not that common; however, many people have some parasitic attachments and these beings can influence people's behavior, thoughts, emotions, and mind states from a distance. There are myriad of these little creatures that can also exist inside people, but in most cases, they influence us by attacking us from outside of the body.

The first step is actually realizing the issue of these entities and being aware that these entities are already part of our reality. The broader context—the true "red pill" understanding that movies such as *The Matrix* and *They Live* communicate—is that these entities have a level of control and power in our reality and that, to varying degrees, we are being farmed. Once you come to terms with that (which is not easy to do), it is actually much better than having your head in the sand and not knowing why the world is the way it is. Once you understand these entities and how they operate, many things about our world and why our world is the way it is make sense, for example, why power corrupts and why people act in such obviously harmful ways to themselves and others.

Viewpoints regarding these malefic beings have traditionally been communicated by the Gnostics related to their understanding of the archons, and these views are completely normalized in most all traditional cultures, whether or not people in these cultures take plant medicines or not. However, for the pseudo-superior Western mind, these ideas can appear heretical, because of the indoctrination about reality inherent in western materialistic viewpoints. The modern globalist paradigm has locked down human minds into limited materialistic modes of thinking (which are often institutionally prejudiced about even entertaining such ideas about reality), and denies that there are unseen layers or levels of reality. Yet, what the media, science, academics, and "skeptics" and all those with some kind authority in culture, is actually beside the point. These beings have been clearly reported by spiritual healers and mystics in the West for many decades, and in pretty much all traditional cultures over thousands of years in almost every society around the world. It is clearly sheer foolishness to be dismissive and not open-minded to the perceptions and practices of people in these cultures. However, this refusal to acknowledge or even entertain these understandings just speaks to us of a clearly captured paradigm.

In some respects, these parasites are mind parasites. They affect how we think and what we feel. They want us to think that what they are thinking is what WE are thinking. If we are not aware of their existence, we can believe we are having a lot of dark and crazy thoughts, or even struggling with self-esteem. Most people can resonate with having unstable or unsettled thoughts, or "dark" intrusive thoughts, that don't even feel like their own. The truth is, one's own thoughts cannot be intrusive, as WE are thinking them; it is only the thoughts of these parasites from outside us which actually can INTRUDE.

A lot of people's dysfunction, issues, and addictions are maintained by these entities. The challenge in clearing them is often that unless the root cause of an issue is addressed, another entity may often simply engage within the individual via the same hole in their psychic armor. You certainly could call these manifestations secondary byproducts of a lack of self-love or self-presence. Once the entity's influence is curtailed then the individual really needs to fill that hollow element within them, with their own presence. In some respects, the extent of the entities overall presence on earth, represents humanity's abdication of its own soul. This abdication appears to emanate from the Western/Roman civilizational blueprint, which has an influence termed *Wetiko* which is an indigenous term explored by Paul Levy in his well-known book "Dispelling Wetiko: Breaking the Curse of Evil".

In this work with psychoactives, we must understand that when opening ourselves up to higher realms, or reaching higher states of consciousness, there can at times be entities wanting to take us down a peg. There is such a phenomenon of people who sustain injuries, such as dissociation and chronic anxiety, through meditation, which is not well understood. However, it would seem to me that what is happening is that people are reaching higher realms or really getting somewhere in their practice and tripping a wire—alerting entities to bring them down a notch. This is because these entities do not want an awakened populace. We can also perceive how many newly spiritually illumined folks initially start off well, then often create circumstances that are dark and cultic in nature. Being human is hard, and in many respects, we are actually at war. If we truly do want to spiritually progress, we must learn how to defeat these entities.

I suppose the mistake I see people making is to treat these beings as anything more than parasites—creating stories about how they are part of the subconscious mind and should be treated with love, and so on and so forth. How you deal with them or relate to them is your story; the first step is in realizing they are a real issue, as much as physical parasites inside the human body (which is, of course, a whole other huge issue) So when we are holding a group space or working with people in general, we want to create a space that prevents these beings from attacking people. This is because, when people are taking strong psychoactives, their ordinary shields are not going to be as strong, and they may be liable to being influenced or even attacked by these beings.

What I see in the ayahuasca space is that many facilitators commonly work with protector beings who help them to protect the space. These beings will sometimes just do this work without even being asked on a conscious level, but you must be working with integrity. Those who do not work with integrity can very often become cultic, trancey, and creepy. Strange things can happen, and their whole show can become co-opted and captured—something not that uncommon in the ayahuasca world. In that case, the space itself becomes more about the entities feeding through the people in the space and interfering with them, rather than about any healing or transformation.

I would say when it comes to being a facilitator, there are levels of initiation—the first one is coming to terms with the existence of these beings and then truly seeing and learning how to deal with them. I think what we will observe in the relatively naive space of mainstream psychedelic psychotherapy, where many folks with "educated" minds cannot stretch into anything like the superstitious or unseen realms, is that it could get very messy. To my mind, the symptoms of overt interference by these entities might be people beginning to act strangely—acts of mysterious sabotage, self-harm, and even suicide, highly manipulative and passive-aggressive, if not just outright aggressive behavior. Such people might also appear somewhat okay on the surface, but on etheric and psychic levels, they are working on behalf of the vampiric agendas of the entities. So then, the blood and efficaciousness is drained from their work, and it looks bloodless and trancelike. The only way that people may know something is wrong is the very distinct feeling something is off. The work then becomes counterproductive when entities have taken it over to siphon off or drain people involved in this work.

I have talked to quite a few people who have perceived parasitic entities that set themselves up in float tank centers, where people are going into a vulnerable, open state of being, where their ordinary shielding is relinquished and their life force is stolen. I have also seen and cleared entities in float tank centers. I think it is important to keep in mind, that the modus operandi of these entities is to remain unseen.

But also, what we will see as awareness increases, are many people actually stepping up and learning how to address these entities. My contribution toward humanity getting together a tactic of addressing these entities is torping. Torping is the name I gave to the high-pitched sound that can kill these entities, which sounds a bit like a dog barking. I developed torping initially just to defend myself in the psychedelic space in 2013, inspired by some walk-ins who talked about a technique they called "boogie busting." In 2021, I learned to torp over people's bodies. Then in 2023, I learned how to do remote torping, where I didn't need to be present with the person. These days, I largely practice remote torping and help people with issues such as sleeplessness, anxiety, psychosis, migraines, intrusive thoughts, depression, catatonia, and general malaise. I have also begun to teach this technique to people.

http://www.torping.com

I would say that a lot of the main reasons why people are reaching for psychedelics is because of some kind of entity interference or another. Psychedelics, in many respects, appear to modulate or regulate the effect that these entities have upon people's energy fields. On some level, psychedelics appear to give the organism a fresh insight into its true, unimpeded functionality. I would say that torping (or any other clearing of entities) will largely become part of humanity's tactic for improving mental health. When we talk about mental health, much of the time the issue with people is simply these parasitic interferences.

Torping can also be integrated into work with people in a one-on-one level and in a group setting. However, it is probably best treated as its own modality, as I would say any spiritual healing modality is. The issue is that you can prevent entities from influencing people, but then other entities will just come back. You need to work with people on their shielding, on their self-love, on their trauma, and deeply into their issues and their life orientation so that there are no openings in their field.

Perhaps what I recommend to practitioners first is to get the torping sound correct. The sound needs to be sharp, forceful, and strong enough-sounding to be appear to be capable of breaking glass. Dogs do it almost correctly, but I doubt most dogs can kill entities—they just ward them off with a sound they intuitively know the entities don't like. The key to making the sound is actually focusing and directing the sound—without doing that, it doesn't work.

The torping sound needs to be expressive and made in the framework of an intention, also. For most people, their issue or complaint is that they don't see the entities. People think that to see the entities, you need to have the ability to have crisp visions in your daily state. Actually, all you need is enough data to be able to target or "lock on" to an interference. That could be a feeling. It could be a sense of opaqueness, a creepy vibe, a blurry circle, or a cartoonish bear. When you begin torping at a sense of opaqueness, it is going to transform, and as you do this, simply let visual impressions occur in your mind. Some of it may be imagination or the brain picking up on a sensation and translating it. For example, you may see all interferences as growling wolves. The brain may put together limited information into something coherent, and that is okay. All you need to do then, is to torp at the growling wolf; and as you do that, you will often see it transform. It can take a bit of time—from 1 minute to 5 minutes, to 10 minutes, and beyond that, even. Don't worry about torping quickly; just get the sound correct and enunciate the sound clearly with an intuitively right pitch.

What will happen when you do this is that the growling wolf (or whatever you are seeing in your minds eye) will change form; ideally, it will kind of melt away or fall down and dissipate. After a time, you will feel that what you are torping at is no longer alive. You might experience an image or animation sequence in your mind or just have a feeling that you are finished. For example, the inner animation might be a referee signaling a knockout with his hands. Again, this might be more like a sensation than a detailed image.

If you want to perhaps see more detailed imagery of entities, then you can take mushrooms or any tryptamine. By just taking psychedelics, you are going to meet interference of certain kinds sooner or later and torping then simply becomes an act of self-defense—so that you don't end up in a really "bad trip" with all your power taken, or in a complete tailspin, or losing your mind in the worst possible way.

However, if you do want to train and develop this sense, probably the best way to go about it is to find some willing, traumatized people, or people who have the classic symptoms of interference, which are poor sleep, intrusive thoughts, anxiety, and headaches. Then you could take a small amount of mushrooms and scan their body. Maybe initially, you can use your hands and see what images come up in your mind. You can also ask the person if they have issues with headaches or pains in parts of their body. Then listen to where the interference is coming from. Then torp that spot in their body and see how they respond, see what you experience. Torp until the interference clears, and then find another spot. Perhaps you will find yourself torping away from the body, at entities who may be quite some distance away.

Traditional work with entities emphasizes the smaller ones that inhabit the body, but my emphasis is on the larger entities that come into the person's field and cause the issues that they experience. Once you start working with somebody, you can begin to look away from their body and hopefully begin to see these entities. This is more advanced work, as before you know it, you may well be in a battle with a lot of entities and hierarchies of entities. Also, you cannot just leave your client after the session. You must follow up with them daily and help them to become clear, usually over 2-3 weeks.

The next step up from working over someone's body is to work remotely with clients, which is not as hard as it may appear once you have the ability to lock onto the entities. You are then less distracted by the physical body and the presence of the person in front of you, so it can be easier to focus on the entities.

Of course, other techniques for clearing entities can be used. Bob Falconer, in his book, *The Others Within Us*, talks about using a technique whereby you are taking the entities back to their source or to the light. This technique originated with the Spiritist Church in Brazil and can work well, but I have my doubts about taking some of these bigger, gnarlier entities to the light. Some people also say they don't believe such entities even belong in the light at all.

A technique called soplar can also be used to deter entities, which is a shooing/fast blowing sound the curanderos in South America use. The entities don't like the blowing of this air toward them and tend to move on. I have found using soplar has limited applicability (apart from not disturbing people with the torping sound), but can work to shoo them away. I've heard other people have different techniques, and I'm sure in the future, people will be aware of many different techniques that can help people be clear of these parasites.

As for how to protect oneself from entities, I think it needs to be a multi-pronged approach. You cannot just rely on one thing, but ultimately, what it comes down to is mental and emotional attitude. Visualizations can also be very powerful. You can use visualizations such as surrounding yourself with a reflective mirror-ball suit of armor radiating white light that reflects negativity. Another primary visualization I use with torping clients is to get them to visualize themselves in a bubble and, with their breath, feel the bubble get stronger. Then visualize another bubble around the primary clear bubble, then a gold bubble, then a silver bubble, and then a white bubble. Then people can say a prayer of protection—one they create is ideal, but a good statement might be: "I command that no negative energies can enter my field without my permission," or "I can create strong protection around me that keeps me safe from anything that might want to harm me." or "I am invisible to all hostile and invasive intent." The issue is that a lot of people have a compromised natural shielding from drugs, alcohol, or trauma, causing them to be anxious and liable to be attacked. These visualizations can help people become consciously aware of their innate shielding and hopefully build it up stronger.

Some people reach back to their heritage in Christianity and find some good prayers there, such as Ephesians 6:10–18 (*The Armour of God*). However, people in the modern day may find these prayers to be full of too much Christian theology. These prayers do have a certain power of morphic resonance and have often been used for centuries. Particularly if you are of

European descent, they would have been used by your lineage, and so there is a power in that. There are many Sanskrit chants which are very specific in dealing with evil spirits—even curses and demons, you can find many of them on YouTube, chanted and repeated for hours. But you can also learn them yourself, and if you are of Indian descent, these chants might well be more potent for you.

I've personally not found crystals to be THAT effective, but I think a lot of their power may be in holding the intention to protect oneself, and if having crystals or stones around that you feel do the job, this might give you confidence or focus to be protected. I know people who work with amulets as well, which they say work to protect them.

Some people also do various things to protect a space, from creating a circle around a space in salt, to visualizations or setting up energetic shielding and protection around a space, or the invocation of certain guardian beings or spirit protectors. Personally, I work with teams of beings who are behind the scenes, that I generally don't interact with—about as much as you might interact with your own hired physical bodyguards, for example.

Each individual must find their own way that works for them. Some people may have relationships with certain higher beings, which is enough. Other people may learn Sanskrit chants, which they feel are sufficient. But in many respects, creating a safe space for people to take psychedelics should come naturally after time. What is most significant is being aware of this issue and taking steps with your actions and intention to create protection and a safe space.

Oftentimes, it may be the entities within people, or already aligned with them, that are going to present themselves into the space. Some people can process their relationships with these entities by themselves or with the plants. Other times, as a facilitator, you may find part of your training is to learn how to help people disattach from these entities. I know a man who was taught in great detail by the teacher plants how to clear entities from people. I prefer to torp them. Everyone has to find their own way, but with focus and intuition, we can find creative ways to support people to eliminate the influence of these parasitic creatures.

Chapter 13

The Presence of Self Work

Probably the most important issue facing people carrying out this work is how to sustainably practice this work and not burn out. On a physical level, this work can look easy. On a metaphysical level however, it can sometimes appear to be the hardest job you could ever do, in terms of the toll and stress it can take on your system.

Our society doesn't yet recognize the mechanisms whereby you can be influenced by other people's "energies." As soon as you are talking about "energies," that for many people may be more "woo" than they can handle. However the absorption of people's emotional states, the engagement with their processing, and the contact with their different levels of traumas and emotional realities can be extremely taxing, in a way that those who have not done this work would generally not be able to comprehend.

However, this effect of feeling drained is perhaps something that introverts can understand, as they can often be drained from regular social circumstances. Yet, even extroverts can find they are drained from this work in a way that is just not comparable to any social situation. I found that when I was holding groups of 15–20 people over 2 nights on a Friday and Saturday night, it felt MUCH worse than any case of jet lag on Sunday and Monday. I would at times feel like I was recovering from a serious bicycle crash. It was usually not until the following Friday that I begin to feel 90% again.

I think there are many reasons why this extreme tiredness happens, and it just depends on your clientele, where they are at, and how you are deciding to interact with them. But as a facilitator, you really should be looking out to protect your energy field as much as possible and not engage too much in other people's energy fields. Overly engaging with people's energy fields means being too close to them for extended periods of time, talking to them too much, too closely, or too intensely, or touching them, or generally tuning into their circumstances too deeply. I have noticed that the people who do burn out (and it definitely is a factor in this work) will be those who tend to engage more with people's energy fields.

On the other hand, you also don't want to be distant, cold, or detached. When having a massage, bodywork, or spiritual healing, there are some practitioners who clearly are avoiding going deep with you. So much so that they do not actually bring about too much healing, as they don't make much contact with you on any truly relevant level.

It is simply not sustainable for individuals to hold space for people 8 hours a day, 40 hours a week. It MIGHT be possible to hold space for 1 person, once a day in a one-on-one session or a two-on-one session that goes for 4 to 6 hours. You certainly could do a group for 2 nights every 2 weeks sustainably, and many ayahuasca facilitators do a big group every month and can sustain that. But people who are in the underground might work with 2 or 3 people a week, at most, 4 people a week. This work, along with pre-brief, integration, and therapy around the session, can really emotionally involve you in people's lives. Therefore, it is important to establish some barriers—for example, to let your client know that their 40 messages in 30 minutes are too many messages for you.

In 2017, I held 10 ayahuasca weekends—Friday and Saturday nights over 12 weeks—with around 15–20 people in each weekend. Towards the end of that time, I was completely cooked—just chronically tired and weary in a profound way. I would need AT LEAST 2 weeks off then, preferably 4 weeks, to arrive back at this work somewhat fresh. Sometimes I have taken 3 to 6 months off from doing this work, until I can return to it fresh and be able to be of useful service.

It is also important to remember that the client's work is theirs to do and that your role as facilitator is to help them, most especially if they are stuck. If they are stuck and when there is not constructive flow in the session, it doesn't take too much to skillfully inspire momentum in most cases. But you also don't want to take over from them and "assist" too much. There clearly is such a thing as an "inner healing intelligence," as the MAPS guide to MDMA psychedelic-assisted therapy manual communicates. Your role is to support and encourage this intelligence, not to override it.

There is also something to be said for holding someone's hand and consoling or comforting them, but perhaps not for more than a few minutes. They must know you are present, but giving them too much consolation is not going to allow them to do the inner work that they must do. We must also watch ourselves and see that we are not imposing ourselves in any way. In most cases, we don't really know the precise state they are in, how it is shifting, and in what exact personal context. Even if it is a one-on-one client and they are telling you in real time what is happening, there is still so much you don't know. I would also not recommend to speak in real time too much, as your client's time is largely best spent going within and focusing on themselves.

To carry out this work on ourselves in the deep self-inquiry that psychoactives bring, we must have at least an understanding of WHY we are doing it. Many people might not understand the essence of their own spiritual journey or what is truly best for them. People can often be entrapped by the mind and ego and don't know in what way they have been ensnared—often in common traps such as spiritual bypassing or thinking they are better than other people because they are "spiritual."

Generally, the people who take psychedelics are those who are willing to "do the work." But after a time, if we are working with the plants or fungi, we know how these agents work with people—what experiences they give, what they like to show people, and how people go through different stages of their journey with the medicine.

A lot of people are in a kind of denial and have

compartmentalized themselves to avoid truly face their own shit. People will do a lot of different things to avoid facing their own shit, including projecting it onto others, or just conveniently bypassing it altogether. Much of the psychedelic, entheogenic, and plant medicine world is oriented toward some sort spiritual bypass or another, and facing your own shit is very hard.

I remember one man who came to one of my retreats in outback Australia who had drunk many dozens of times with many ayahuascaros, but it had all been about spiritual experiences for him—such as talking to aliens and Jesus. So when he did drink a couple of times on the retreat, another retreat participant said it was as if he had never drank ayahuasca before. That was because he was having to face his own shit and address his own real issues, rather than completely immerse himself into the visions or the transcendent.

There are many things facilitators can do that can distract people from their own inner work. To my mind, TOO MUCH focus on ceremony, singing songs or dancing also doesn't allow people to go that deep. Again, you really need to give people space to face their own challenges and find a way to both sit with their pain and then also to deal with it. As the facilitator, you should know what it is like to feel stuck with yourself with no way out, as a fuck-up drenched in your own shit, shamed and full of mess, strife, and bad life choices (which, of course, we all have). People so often forget that these medicines very often bring up what is not working for us.

If everything is working out fine while we are "journeying," then we're not truly facing our problems at their root. It can be challenging to admit one's weaknesses, faults, and deficiencies, but if we can do so and not deny them, a sense of self-acceptance and self-love can come into the picture. To my mind, we need to be clear about our own weaknesses so that we can become more secure in ourselves. As facilitators, if we are all puffed up and appear totally with it and sorted, this can be triggering to people, as they see this attitude in the world commonly, and it looks like denial. People also may then become unconsciously resentful and may begin to be triggered in counterproductive ways. People who put themselves up on a pedestal must deal with inevitably falling off it, also. People can begin to idealize you as a father or mother figure they never had. We are better off being in a space of showing up in our weaknesses, being honest about them, and making fun of ourselves.

You really do want to be disarming people, rather than appearing like some mighty, immovable rock. Society generally rewards people who APPEAR solid, rather than the people who admit inner inconsistencies. Security must come from within; it cannot be faked, and security comes from truly "knowing oneself." But that security is multifaceted. It should mean that we have a good idea of how we appear to others and the kinds of things they may think about us. We should also largely know what people find challenging about interacting with us, what people may like and dislike about us, and have come to terms with that.

A lot of people are not integrated within themselves; most people have this huge array of personal history they haven't accounted for or processed. This is why "the wounded healer" is often the best healer—as they can empathize with how "fucked up" people can be and have compassion for others. Sometimes it might be worth remembering that many of the people we are working with are new to even truly looking at themselves. It is worth reflecting on your own personal process—what it was like for you to face this expandedness, and to remember how long it took for you to integrate this new spaciousness and what you found challenging in that process. It is worth keeping in mind how messy and discombobulated you felt—how confronting and perhaps embarrassing it was to begin to confront all of this personal material. How difficult it may have been to acknowledge the transpersonal truth and how ontologically challenging it was to also recognize this wonder and what it was like to become entranced by the visions and lure of apparent spiritual knowledge.

We also have to generally account for people's different belief systems and approaches to life. After a time, we begin to understand patterns in people and recognize how they will respond. But in general, the people who are willing to do this work are of a different level than the average person on the street, as they are largely willing to face up to reality. We need to give people credit, support, and encouragement, and realize how difficult it can be to confront the paradoxes and inconsistencies within. One of my helpers would often say to people, "You're doing so well!" to encourage them.

I think it is true that these medicines can help us to understand what self-work is, and what truly facing up to reality in all its facets can be. The plants can also guide you to change your relating to your own patterns, so processes of self-work you do in the medicine space can be enlivened in your daily life.

For many people, how they have constructed themselves in relation to their environment—as a personality, as a mind, an ego, or a psyche—is all that they have. It is their sense of identity that they rabidly hold onto. We cannot underestimate how confronting and terrifying this "ego death" is for many people. We cannot underestimate that feeling of being in the abyss and the feeling of being about to go mad. We cannot underestimate how confronting it is to have one's views about reality and life shattered. It is very difficult to give up so many illusions and ideas that we might have had. It is not easy to realize how programmed we all are, and how wrong and backwards so many things are that we ourselves may have subscribed to. It is hard to give up identities when, throughout your life, you have felt that these identities represent who you really are. Change doesn't come easily to many people, and there are good reasons for that.

We cannot underestimate how hard it is for people to truly "get their arse kicked." It is ten times more humiliating than one of your parents dressing you down, as you generally cannot protest at all. Admitting where you are wrong is often necessary for growth, but there is not very much in our society that facilitates a process where this type of change can occur.

We also cannot underestimate just how difficult it is for your average person to deal with their shadow—and with the entities that affect them with dark and crazy thoughts, which they generally are unwilling to share and acknowledge. This is the loneliness of much of the populace. They themselves are often acting against themselves and other people, and may want to change, but cannot. Some people are caught up in circumstances, whole careers, or businesses involving many others, where they may be causing more harm than good. Some people have been caught up in cults, where they may have been complicit in the abuse and mistreatment of others. We cannot underestimate the karma of people's lies and deceptions, or how they judge and condemn themselves. We cannot underestimate the well of self-hatred, doubt, and insecurity that many people face on a daily basis, all the while trying to present a brave face to the world. We cannot underestimate people's suffering—or the shock of being in shock, in a state of numbness, unable or unwilling to feel the extent of how damaged, denuded, and confused their internal landscape truly is.

Again and again, we just need to come back to realizing that we cannot know all that much about what people are going through—in their experience or in their lives. Over time, we can begin to understand the general flavor and tenor of most people's experiences and processes, but the best thing we can do is to give them space, offer them a gentle ear, and allow their own intelligence—and the medicine—to bring them back to increased alignment with themselves.

Ayahuasca understands that some people need to be seduced. She'll give some people rapturous, cosmic, blissful experiences for maybe the first few times, and then after a while, the deep, dark work of investigating the shadow will begin. But if these people were given the raw deep work to begin with in their first experiences, they would have run away and never come back. Some other people need to get results first off. They need to go right into their trauma, and they might have a difficult journey, but they will get incredible results, and be ready to go back in, willingly.

Being human is often difficult. Not everyone is up to the challenge, it seems. These medicines give people a chance to change and transform, but they are in no way a panacea for human life. Most of the people who say they are some sort of spiritual shortcut just don't have much experience with them. As if the presumed "destination" were just around the corner and easy to reach with a bit of psychotropic assistance.

There are many modalities, techniques, and processes that some people will need to combine with psychedelic medicine in order to truly get results. A foundation of profound self-reflection is something that must come from within. Through the use of psychedelic medicine, not everyone is going to magically transform into someone whose conduct is appropriate, kind or even sane. The individual must be embedded within their own patient self-awareness and self-work, on all levels of their being—physical, spiritual, emotional, and mental—if they truly do desire positive transformation.

Chapter 14

World Views and What Helps

At the time of writing this book in 2026, the Western world is still primarily oriented to a rather limited worldview that only considers the physical world to be real and anything that cannot be measured is not considered real by science. Yet, there are some significant and articulate figures in the West who have explored, documented, and understood the existence of other realities beyond the presumed material dimension.

For example, Stan Grof, who pioneered transpersonal psychology with LSD psychotherapy and Holotropic Breathwork, engaged in very expanded worldviews explained in his many books. Wilhelm Reich was perhaps the first person in the West to understand that psycho-pathology existed within the body and that there was an invisible energy that could be measured, which he called Orgone. Barbara Ann Brennan discovered that there were energy fields that interacted between people, and attempted to map the human energy in a way appropriate to science in the 1990s. Terence McKenna spoke of the mystery of the tryptamines, and that there were other greater and wider realities beyond ours. Certainly, Robert A. Monroe did the same thing, communicating of a greater reality beyond the physical realm, catalyzed by his *Hemi-Sync* tapes, rather than via psychedelics. People such as Ken Wilber communicate of greater realities beyond the physical, synthesizing Eastern and Western viewpoints.

In our time, people like Bob Falconer, Jerry Marzinsky, and myself have been publicly communicating to people regarding the existence of etheric parasites—independently coming to largely the same conclusions. And there are many deep explorers and practitioners who are not public communicators. The point is, there are wider realities—spiritual realities, not just physical realities—which by any measure, is the logical conclusion to have about reality itself.

Mainstream Western viewpoints are still embedded within centuries-old philosophical traditions, which maintain that the way to understand the world is through the mind rather than any kind of direct experience. In many respects, the dogma of religion itself still has a hold over the Western psyche—and any mode of understanding that directly threatens the now rather ghostlike, but still present power of the church, tends to be snubbed within culture.

When dealing with clients, we must know how to gently reorient them in their belief systems, as their worldview is innately expanded and opened up. We might deal with clients who grew up within a strict religious setting. We might have clients who are complete atheistic materialists, yet these viewpoints can also change—and commonly do.

One of the primary advantages of these mind medicines is seeing the limitations of fixed belief systems and the issues involved in isolating oneself within these fixed viewpoints, which perceive reality in a limited and deterministic manner. We cannot presume to, in any way, indoctrinate or inculcate people into any kind of belief system. But there are some things that experience proves to be evident—such as the existence of plant spirits and other realms of existence. It is so common for people to come to me with their stories, which they think might surprise me. Most of the time, I've heard it before or something very similar, and I tell them it is another day at the office for me.

It is certainly not our role as facilitators to indoctrinate or introduce "our teachings" to people. I remember when drinking ayahuasca with the now-deceased young ayahuascaro Kevin Furnas in Iquitos. He would talk for quite some time about past lives and what I thought were quite dogmatic views of the soul's journey.

Then again, we do need to be able to guide people. We need to empower them to find their own answer or meet the mystery on its own terms. As humans, it would appear we're not given access passes to all the mysteries of the universe. Many of us have had the experience of grasping something of fundamental importance deep within our experiences and then having it pulled away from us or erased from memory as we emerge back into our regular mind and body state. I'd say it is rare that people take psychedelics and return to their religious roots, although it certainly does happen—that people suddenly have a spiritual experience and then return to the apparent simplicity of their inherited religious tradition.

The human mind can be a bit overwhelmed by all the tools, techniques, and modalities out there. I'd say that it ultimately doesn't matter what the modality is, but that about 90% of people who practice any modality are just not that capable as healers. Plus, there is so much out there in terms of techniques and processes, viewpoints, and "shamans"—people can bounce between one healer or another and some inconsequential things that may or may not work very well.

I'm a big believer in all things bodywork and massage —not as a way of relaxing, but as a means of balancing and aligning the body, and therefore the mind. There is just a lot of tension that the muscles hold, and almost everyone is tense and holding in their body. Bodywork is a brilliant medium to keep up circulation, get the lymph system moving, and align the body's systems. I personally try to get some bodywork once a month at least, preferably once a week, if I'm in a place where I can find someone good. This is the challenge, I find: there is a massive gulf between the very good and the just average.

I've had huge shifts with spiritual healing in my life, particularly with those who have trained at the Barbara Ann Brennan School of Spiritual Healing. I believe that the shifts created by a good spiritual healer can equal those of working with a plant medicine healer.

Breathwork in general can be very helpful. It is something you need to practice a bit so that it becomes easy to do and not a strain. To start off with, people might need to see a practitioner or do breathwork in a group so they can get good at it and have some breakthroughs with it. But after a time, you can just do it yourself. I simply just breathe in and out quickly through my mouth which, to me, is just the natural technique my body defaults to. And I find doing breathwork whilst taking psychedelics is like rocket fuel for the psychedelic state.

I think that Internal Family Systems is where therapy becomes truly effective and shows us that we humans are a lot more complex than we think we may be—made up of many different parts. Anyone could benefit from 5 or so sessions of Internal Family Systems with a good therapist, so they can learn to listen to their different parts. I do think that IFS also needs to be somatic and not just head-based, and that integrating this understanding with the body is a very good idea.

Kinesiology is one of those things that can be very good if you can find a good practitioner, and very much below average if you have an average practitioner. Acupuncture is great if you can find an adventurous acupuncturist who can traverse beyond the basics of so-called Traditional Chinese Medicine, in which case it may become transformative.

I believe in taking plants and all kinds of herbs as a tonic for the body. Most kinds of herbalism or herbs that I have engaged with, I have found to be beneficial. I, myself, like to take plants and herbs regularly, and I find the issue is often in finding quality herbal products, as many commercial herbs are diluted or compromised in some way.

I am also a big fan of flower essences—perhaps not so much the Bach remedies, but definitely the American

Flower Essence Services range, the Alaskan Essences range, and the Flora of Asia range. I also make them myself. Whatever our psychological, spiritual, or mental condition, there is a flower essence that can help. Many of the flower essences can shift energies, loops, and emotional states very quickly and succinctly. I also like to make flower essence blends for my clients to take after a session.

Then there are endemic issues in the terrain of our society. For example, many people's diets may create an imbalance in their gut. I pretty much recommend Bravo Yogurt to everyone—a yogurt that contains 300 bacterial strains which are very good for gut health and serious issues in the gut. The Bravo suppositories are also very good.

A lot of people have parasites and issues with their gut that are labeled all kinds of things, such as Crohn's disease or Irritable Bowel Syndrome. However, they just might have physical parasites or an issue with biofilm. Biofilm is a substance that these parasites and bacteria create out of toxins, to protect themselves and trick the immune system into not addressing the imbalance in the digestive system. Addressing the biofilm is tricky, and for most people, they would do well to find a specialist in this area who can help them to clear pathogens and biofilm in their body.

I have found that by keeping my nose to the ground of culture and trying almost everything related to human health and healing, I have come to understand the latest techniques and processes that can help people. You can often see that some people need to get out of their heads and into their bodies. It is not difficult to recommend something to your clients that you think they would be interested in doing.

But a lot of people haven't got the fundamentals down. Their diet is poor, they drink the toxic tap water and 12 cups of coffee a day, and they work in a job they hate. I personally find myself talking to people about livelihood a lot. Many people are not happy with their livelihood. They often don't have a good awareness that many of the things around them are toxic and can harm them. I try to guide people without being dictatorial.

I remember many years ago, a friend of mine gave his friend changa, and from that one experience, he went from only eating McDonald's and drinking Coke all the time to drinking juices and eating healthily. People essentially know what is good for them, and it is not our role to tell them, as they'll often come to it when it is right for them.

A lot of people in our sub-optimal society find it difficult to be social beings. Considering that we are wired as social beings, this difficulty can negatively affect our well-being. Western society doesn't have much of a good or healthy ethos of relationships and interpersonal respect. Many people find it more expedient to lock themselves away and not interact with others, which is not ultimately good for one's mental health.

As a facilitator, you are working with both people and medicines, which are two of the most potent agents of change. Connecting to others—in intimacy or community—is often going to be the biggest medicine for people to understand our essential unity and for people to understand that they are not alone, that they share many of the same struggles and issues with other human beings.

Each of us human beings has the potential to provide the most powerful medicine to each other, and it is often that through these plant medicines by which we can truly understand how we can be people who can heal others through the presence of our humanity.

Bibliography

Berceli, D. (2008). *Trauma releasing exercises (TRE): A revolutionary new method for stress/trauma recovery*. Namaste Publishing.

Brennan, B. A. (1987). *Hands of light: A guide to healing through the human energy field*. Bantam Books.

Brennan, B. A. (1993). *Light emerging: The journey of personal healing*. Bantam Books.

Falconer, R. (2012). *The others within us: Internal family systems, porosity, and multiple mind*. Karnac Books.

Grof, S. (2008). *LSD psychotherapy* (4th ed.). MAPS.

Hancock, G. (2005). *Supernatural: Meetings with the ancient teachers of mankind*. Disinformation.

Levy, P. (2013). *Dispelling Wetiko: Breaking the curse of evil*. North Atlantic Books.

Marzinsky, J. (2019). *An amazing journey into the psychotic mind: Breaking the spell of the ivory tower*. Inner Traditions.

Mithoefer, M., Mithoefer, A., Jerome, L., Ruse, J., Doblin, R., Gibson, E., Ot'alora, M. G., & Sola, E. (2017). *Treatment manual: MDMA-assisted therapy for PTSD* (Version 8.1). Multidisciplinary Association for Psychedelic Studies.

Monroe, R. A. (1985). *Far journeys*. Doubleday.

Palmer, J. (2014). *Articulations: On the utilisation and meanings of psychedelics*. Anastomosis Books.

Pierrakos, J. C. (1987). *Core energetics: Developing the capacity to love and heal*. Mendocino Press.

Schwartz, R. C. (1995). *Internal family systems therapy*. Guilford Press.

Strassman, R. (2001). *DMT: The spirit molecule*. Park Street Press.

www.ingramcontent.com/pod-product-compliance
Ingram Content Group UK Ltd.
Pitfield, Milton Keynes, MK11 3LW, UK
UKHW062305290726
14090UKWH00018B/895

9 780992 552855